CONSERVATIVE VOTES, LIBERAL VICTORIES

CONSERVATIVE VOTES, LIBERAL VICTORIES

Why the Right Has Failed

PATRICK J. BUCHANAN

Quadrangle / The New York Times Book Co.

Designed by Tere LoPrete

Library of Congress Cataloging in Publication Data

Buchanan, Patrick J
    Conservative votes, liberal victories.

    Includes bibliographical references and index.
    1. Conservatism—United States. 2. Liberalism
—United States. 3. United States—Politics and
government—1869–1974. 4. United States—Politics
and government—1974. I. Title.
JA84.U5B78   320.5'0973   75-8302
ISBN 0-8129-0582-2

Contents

☆

Acknowledgments

Though they will deny it under oath, several editors and officials of *The New York Times*—at a luncheon in the fall of 1974—provided me with the idea and the encouragement to write this slim book.

The chapters which follow, however, represent my own reflections on a question that constantly troubles the American right: why the conservative sentiment in the country so rarely translates into conservative government in the capital. The principal source of the thoughts, arguments and views expressed herein is my own experience in Mr. Nixon's White House from 20 January 1969 to 8 August 1974.

In analyzing that experience, however, I have drawn on the thinking and writing of a small community of scholars whom the national press has separated into schools of political thought variously identified as traditional conservative, neo-conservative, and populist conservative. Among the two dozen authors whose books were hauled off to Key Biscayne, where this volume was outlined and drafted, and who may recognize their own positions adumbrated in Buchanan's prose are Jeffrey Hart, Kevin Phillips, Richard Whalen, Edward Epstein, William F. Buckley, Jr., Edward Banfield, Roger Freeman and Irving Kristol, four of them former colleagues, all of them current friends.

Reading these chapters, they may, especially Professor Kristol, the most referenced man in the book, understand what it was J. Alfred Prufrock was trying to say when he toyed with the line:

> That is not it at all
> That is not what I meant at all

A special debt is owed to Roger Freeman and Lyndon (Mort) Allin, former Special Assistants to the former President, who read drafts of the book, and whose comments and criticism were valued and incorporated in the final manuscript. Finally, a word of appreciation to Teresa Rhodes Rosenberger of The White House research staff for her many hours of assistance, and a volume of gratitude to my wife, Shelley, who contributed as many hours of effort as the author.

PATRICK J. BUCHANAN
Washington, D.C.
4 July, 1975

CONSERVATIVE
VOTES,
LIBERAL
VICTORIES

☆

Introduction

At the high watermark of the Nixon Presidency, as the White House and Mr. Agnew were hurling their rhetorical thunderbolts down upon the cohorts of the political left, Senate Minority Leader Hugh Scott consoled his fretting liberal colleagues, "The conservatives get the rhetoric," he observed, and "we get the action."

Il n'y a que la vérité qui blesse. It is only the truth that hurts.

Men of the right, conservatives, captured the Republican Party in the raucous coup at the San Francisco Cow Palace in the summer of '64. They have controlled it since. In 1968, Mr. Nixon owed his nomination to the party's conservative wing, not the dwindling Dewey-Rockefeller forces. Had Senators Goldwater, Tower and Thurmond broken to Ronald Reagan at that convention in Miami Beach, Richard Nixon would have been denied nomination on the first ballot.

In 1972 it was the social conservative, George Wallace, who dominated the Democratic primaries, until he was shot down in a Laurel, Maryland, shopping center. And it was a conservative issues campaign against the candidate of the liberal wing of the Democratic Party that gave Mr. Nixon the greatest landslide won by a genuine Republican in fifty years.

Yet, with all the conservative primary, convention and election victories of the last decade, with the polls showing a national drift to the right, conservative influence upon public policy in America has been pitifully small. Conservatives have failed utterly to translate political support and ballot victories into national policy.

The author's reflections upon that failure led to this book. One needs some answer to the question of why it is true of conservatives politically what Malraux said of Americans generally: that they "make war so well and peace so badly."

Surely, it would be false to suggest that Richard Nixon's victories were without meaning for the nation, or the right wing of American politics. Had Richard Nixon not been in the Oval Office, American policy would have collapsed half a decade before it finally did in Southeast Asia. The line would not have been drawn so soon or so firmly against the political extremism of the sixties. Among Mr. Nixon's signal achievements was to ring down the curtain upon that dreadful era, culminating in 1968, of campus disorders, urban riots, domestic turmoil and political assassination. For the cooling of America, he deserves the commendation of history. And even his greatest adversaries will concede that without the thirty-seventh President of the United States, the Supreme Court would be a different institution.

Yet, looking back at the budget, economic and social policies of the Republican years, it would not be unfair to conclude that the political verdict of 1968 had brought reaffirmation, rather than repudiation, of Great Society liberalism.

The old programs and the older agencies to be dismantled endured; they easily survived Mr. Nixon. The redistribute-the-wealth philosophy still informs federal policy; the egalitarian and integrationist impulses are more prevalent than ever at HEW, Justice and Labor. The unbalanced federal budget is as much a trademark of the administrations of

Nixon and Ford as of Kennedy and Johnson. The defense portion of the federal budget continues to decline; and the welfare state expands, at every level, in authority, numbers, wealth and size to dwarf anything dreamed up by the professors Franklin Roosevelt brought along to Washington.

Indeed, the conservative rhetoric of the victorious campaigns of 1968 and 1972 is wholly misleading, if one wishes to understand the domestic and economic policies of the Republican years.

In his brief statement of conviction, *The Conscience of a Conservative*, published in 1960, Senator Barry Goldwater warned of the inexorable growth of a federal government whose "spending is now approaching a hundred billion dollars a year."[1] A decade and a half later, Senator Goldwater and some who entered politics under his banners were, bayonets fixed, manning the last defenses of a Republican president under whom federal spending was reaching $300 billion a year.

Why is it, one conservative intellectual has asked aloud, that whenever one of our friends reaches a position to do us some good, he ceases to be one of our friends?

This brief volume is written then to explain, at least in part, why policy does not move in a conservative direction, regardless of the outcome at the ballot box. Among its purposes is the identification and description of those obstacles which prevent the implementation of any conservative mandate into conservative government.

Know thy enemy, know thyself; in a thousand battles, a thousand victories. So said Sun Tzu twenty-three centuries ago. It remains wise counsel for politicians as well as generals.

Within the book, several issues are separately addressed. Among them is a phenomenon of interest to essayists for generations: the traditional hostility of the Western intelligentsia toward the capitalist system. A quarter of a century ago, a symposium of the Mont Pélèrin Society held at Beauvallon in France addressed the question. In his contribution, Bertrand de Jouvenel stated as fact: "An enormous majority of Western intellectuals display and affirm hostility to the economic and social institutions of their society, institutions to which they give the blanket name of capitalism."[2]

Why this is so and the implications of this hostility in an era of mass communication and mass education are of importance in understanding the nature of political conflict, at the outset of America's third century.

Another issue addressed is the influence of the nation's media monopolies upon the political process. There is more truth than wit in Oscar Wilde's observation that, "In America the President reigns for four years and journalism governs forever and ever." The nation has passed through in the last dozen years what Kevin Phillips and others have characterized as a "communications revolution." And in this observer's mind, it is still an unsettled question whether political democracy can survive a situation where two-thirds of the citizenry now depend upon, as the primary source of their news and information about government, society and the world, a medium with the peculiar demands of network television.

The comments herein on race and politics will be adjudged among the most mean-spirited of a thoroughly ill-tempered book. To criticize moderate black leaders, to oppose their demands for the use of federal authority to bring about racial integration, is still beyond the pale in Washington politics. Yet, the issue needs to be confronted, for the fabric of American society is being torn apart.

Like no other in public life, the race issue is suffused with hypocrisy. Rarely do upper-middle-class bureaucrats and judges live in the neighborhoods or send their children to the public schools which bear the brunt of the integration plans drafted to soothe their tormented social consciences. The national Republicans and the national Democrats have done nothing to meet the angry and legitimate complaints of working- and middle-class ethnic Americans who have to pay the price of the reverse discrimination which is rapidly calcifying into federal policy. And there is a storm building in America.

After waiting for what seemed like hours for the Reverend Ralph David Abernathy to appear at a scheduled press conference in Miami Beach in 1968, Norman Mailer gave voice to an emotion hundreds of thousands today feel, with far greater justification:

> . . . as the minutes went by and the annoyance mounted, the reporter became aware after a while of a curious emotion in himself, for he had not ever felt it consciously before—it was a simple emotion and very unpleasant to him—he was getting tired of Negroes and their rights. It was a miserable recognition, and on many a count, for if he felt even a hint this way, then what immeasurable tides of rage must be loose in America itself.[3]

A century after the first ended, the time has come to drop the curtain on the Second Reconstruction.

Turning to foreign policy, where even the former President's avowed enemies conceded him a measure of praise, the comments within will be read, not unfairly, as reflecting profound disbelief in the durability and wisdom of detente. So they do.

One hopes that Mr. Nixon's ambitions for detente, his oft-predicted dream of a "generation of peace" will be realized. More hinges upon it than simply his own and Dr. Kissinger's place in history. Still, that hope requires a continuing suspension of disbelief impossible to maintain in the face of what daily transpires in the world.

Years back, Leon Trotsky warned that those who wanted a tranquil existence should not have chosen to be born in the twentieth century. There is no evidence to suggest that the last quarter of that century will be any less dangerous than the preceding three.

Still, one may be a critic and skeptic of detente with the Soviets and Chinese and still admire the skill with which Mr. Nixon and Dr. Kissinger pursued their three-cornered game with the Communist powers, as well as the tenacity and courage with which the President held on, in Southeast Asia, against immense opposition and considerable odds. Had the cancer of Watergate not fatally diseased his Presidency in the spring of 1973, the ultimate disaster would surely have been postponed for years, if not averted altogether.

Yet history judges a nation's foreign policy by the success with which it is crowned, not by the skill and brilliance with which it is pursued. And it must be conceded that the Nixon Presidency did not halt America or the West's strategic retreat from the world, the end of which is not yet remotely in sight.

Where does the political right go from here?

Has the Republican vessel been so severely damaged in the Watergate battering that it is no longer seaworthy? Should conservatives risk the election of a liberal Democrat in 1976 by throwing their support to a third party challenge to the Republicans?

The answers to such questions, fateful ones for the party, the conservatives and the country, cannot be delayed forever.

Nevertheless, some things may be said.

The right must recognize the truth of John F. Kennedy's observation that "sometimes party loyalty asks too much." The traditional party discipline of conservatives, behind their President, has too often been maintained at the expense of principles and policies in which we believe.

Conservatives should seek out, not avoid, political conflict with liberals of both parties, on issues, domestic and foreign. We have nothing to lose by confrontation politics. The nation is a divided country; but it was not divided by conservatives; and it should not be our business to compromise our principles, to silence our complaints, or to abandon our point of view to "bring us together." If the right has a purpose in American politics, it is not to contribute to some false sense of unity, but to articulate the concerns, represent the interests and defend the principles, values and beliefs of our own. In the title of Richard Whalen's book, our business is "taking sides."

☆

Why Liberalism Prevails

Three years ago, one George McGovern was heard to declare that, if nominated by the Democrats, his candidacy would provide Americans with "the clearest choice in a century." And so it did.

Face-to-face with the undiluted dogma of the national Democrats, the nation fled to Mr. Nixon and Mr. Agnew, leaving the Prairie Populist and his frenetic accomplice to dig themselves out from under an earthslide of 47 million votes.

Two years later, the Democrats would not repeat the errors of '72. In the fall elections of 1974 clearly defined positions were consciously avoided. Mr. McGovern, whom *Newsweek* once termed the "closest thing to an ideological radical" ever to run for the Presidency, surfaced in South Dakota, self-christened a "new conservative." In Colorado, Gary Hart managed to win a Senate seat by getting around to the right of Peter Dominick. And Birch Bayh, running successfully for a third term in Indiana, crusaded against fiscal irresponsibility. Hart, McGovern and Bayh—a less likely trio of Treasury watchdogs can scarcely be imagined.

Yet, it was a politic piece of duplicity, and the ruse succeeded. The Democratic revival of 1974 was accomplished by exploiting the rhetoric of the victors of '72.

Still, there was a hollowness to the triumph. The Democrats had carried Congress by condemning fiscal policies they had themselves employed for nearly forty years. They had failed to capture the imagination of the country, for some New Frontier or Great Society program. Indeed, they had offered no program. They had not won the confidence of the country; the Republicans had lost it.

Disgusted with the party in power, unenthusiastic about the alternative, 62 percent of the nation's voters, largest majority in twenty-eight years, stayed home. Some 47 million had given Richard Nixon and the Republicans the Mandate of 1972. The "mandate" of the Ninety-fourth Congress, about which the Democrats chattered and chirped, was built on the ballots of 30 million Americans, only a handful more than voted for George McGovern and Sargent Shriver.

To the political liberal, democracy is a religious faith; and the failure to vote akin to missing one's Easter duty. Thus, the 38 percent turnout in November of 1974 produced consternation and disquiet on the left.

Nor are the explanations advanced adequate. Watergate, we are told, induced a general distrust of all politicians; and hence millions heeded the proverbial counsel of the little old lady who said, "I never vote; it only encourages them."

This may help explain why fewer than two in five voted in 1974; it does not explain why participation in federal elections has been falling, consistently, for a decade.

For that phenomenon, there are simpler explanations, closer at hand. After Vietnam, Americans no longer really believe what the Government says, and after all the utopian nonsense and overblown rhetoric of the New Frontier and Great Society, they no longer believe politicians can or will deliver what they promise. There is a pervasive cynicism about democracy abroad in the land.

Millions are concluding that the political process is meaningless in terms of influencing policy. No matter the politicians elected to office, the policies against which they protest remain the same. This sentiment explains the diminishing voter turnouts, the rising number who declare themselves "independent," and the growing number who express "no interest whatsoever" in politics. And these voters are not without historical justification for feeling and thinking as they do.

In 1964, by statewide referendum, Californians approved a law guaranteeing freedom of choice in the sale of their homes to prospective buyers. The California Supreme Court reversed that democratic decision, and repealed the law. In 1972, voters in North Dakota and Michigan, responding to a grass roots campaign by the right-to-life movement, outlawed abortion on demand as contravening their belief in the sanctity of human life. The Supreme Court mooted those decisions.

In state after state, voters have endorsed candidates and propositions favoring reinstatement of the death penalty for capital crimes. Yet, since the last decade, despite tens of thousands of homicides, not a single convicted criminal has paid with his life for the lives taken. Richard Speck and Charles Manson are today being fed, clothed, sheltered, and presumably rehabilitated on the tax dollars of the families and friends of those they indiscriminately slaughtered.

Since the Warren Court outlawed prayer in the public schools, surveys have shown Americans supporting a constitutional amendment if necessary to restore it. But no prayer amendment will emanate from this Congress. And the parables of Christ remain prohibited in the same high schools where the racist drivel of Eldridge Cleaver is deemed to be "relevant."

The more insistent the public becomes that courts mete out harsher punishment to the criminal class, the more "progressive" and "permissive" are our judges. The more disheartened parents become over the smut that has made American culture a veritable Lake Erie, the less that is attempted, the less that is done. What would have had a distributor jailed ten years ago is now showing at the neighborhood theatre. Tomorrow, one may be certain, the commercial networks will have it edited "tastefully" for prime time.

Consider bussing. If there exists a social policy upon which Americans are united in hostility, it is this totalitarian practice of forcibly transporting children away from homes and neighborhoods across whole cities to conform with some assistant secretary's concept of what is an acceptable racial balance. That hostility has been manifest in polls and surveys, in interviews and election boxes, in demonstrations and disorder. To what avail? Indifferent to the election returns, contemptuous of the sentiments, values and beliefs of the vast majority, the ideologues at HEW continue to draw up their plans, and the federal judges to hand down their decrees, while a cowardly Congress passes toothless resolutions expressing its dismay with forced bussing.

"Send them a message," demanded the Governor of Alabama in the primaries of '72. By the hundreds of thousands, Democrats, who shared Wallace's indignation at high taxes and forced bussing, and his contempt for "guidelines" crafted and imposed by a distant, arrogant bureaucracy, responded. With little organization and less planning, Wallace swept aside the bally-hooed "new politics" of George McGovern and the bread-and-butter liberalism of Hubert Humphrey in Florida, Tennessee, North Carolina, Michigan and Maryland. Weeks after he had been shot down in a Laurel, Maryland, shopping center, and was lying near death in a Silver Spring hospital, Wallace led the Democratic field in popular votes. The message was sent by the social conservatives of the Democratic Party. Was it received? Inquire of the Irish in South Boston.

Nor does the Republican White House merit general absolution. The "guaranteed annual income" against which candidate Nixon railed in the primaries of '68 was embraced as policy by President Nixon in the summer of '69—artfully disguised as the Family Assistance Plan. The strategic "superiority" over the Soviets, indispensable to the national security in '68, was jettisoned for "sufficiency" in 1969, for "parity" in 1971 and for inferiority in missiles and throw-weight, written into the text of Salt I, signed at Moscow, May, 1972.

Those "wasteful social programs" against which we penned

our polemics in the campaign of 1968 were transformed into "spending for human resources" in the presidential messages of 1971 and 1972. Vigorously did we inveigh against the Great Society; enthusiastically did we fund it. LBJ's last budget proposed $73 billion for Great Society social spending; the final budget of Mr. Nixon earmarked $150 billion for the same programs. Hard upon our taking office, the caterpillars and frogs of the campaign of '68 became butterflies and princes.

Deploring the economic policies of his predecessors, Mr. Nixon declared in 1968, "The international monetary crisis is the result of a half decade of fiscal and monetary irresponsibility on a scale unprecedented in the nation's history. A primary and undeniable cause of the current crisis is the uninterrupted string of budget deficits run by this administration, which have added nearly $50 billion to the national debt in five years."[1] Under the President who handed up that indictment, there were two dollar devaluations, and more than $66 billion was added to the national debt.

In the campaign of 1972, three of the issues upon which the White House rallied the new majority where racial quotas, amnesty, and new taxes. Uncompromising and adamant opposition fairly describes the positions we assumed.

In the next two years, the Department of HEW of the same administration which had sworn eternal hostility toward quotas was imposing them on dozens of college faculties, under the euphemism, "numerical goals and timetables." And President Nixon's furniture was not out of the Oval Office sixty days before President Ford had declared a limited amnesty, and was beseeching his former congressional colleagues to impose a 5-percent surtax upon the very businessmen and middle-class voters who had returned the Republicans to power on a pledge of "no new taxes."

Americans are taking a holiday from the democratic rituals because they have come to realize that the ballot box is a device whereby one may alter the composition of the cast, but not the script.

Under both parties in the last dozen years we have had

huge deficits and consequent inflation. Under both parties, the military strength of the United States has declined relative to the Soviet Union. Under both parties, compulsory integration has been forced upon recalcitrant schools, neighborhoods and communities. Under both parties, government has prospered and grown apace. No Administration seems to believe its legacy to the nation is complete without a handful of new agencies or departments as monuments to mark its passage.

"There's not a dime's worth of difference between 'em," Governor Wallace used to say. It is not difficult to understand the appeal of the argument. To conservatives, the on-going squabbles between Republicans and Democrats often seem of little more consequence than the political rupture Swift's Gulliver encountered on arrival in Lilliput. It seems the little empire was steeped in civil war, lasting some "six and thirty moons," between the Big-Endians and the Little-Endians, the genesis of the quarrel being a dispute over which end of the egg should be cracked first, before eating.

Late last February, political columnist David Broder analyzed the respective positions of Republicans and Democrats and came away with the conclusion that there were indeed deep and fundamental disagreements between the parties. Republicans, he wrote, are concerned about the profit squeeze on business; they want restraint and discipline in federal spending; they want a cap on social programs. The unanswered question is why Federal policy has moved in the opposite direction, at an accelerating rate of speed, even after two national Republican victories—the last being the greatest landslide in the history of the Party.

Why Americans, by the millions, "go fishing" on election day is less difficult to understand than why the sentiments expressed at the ballot box are so rarely translated into public policy.

In the decade past, when "the finest generation of young people we have ever produced," was conducting its unstructured street activities, handing down its "non-negotiable demands," those in office were warned, *ad nauseam*, by the Lords Spiritual that our institutions, policies and programs must be responsive to the children. Why is the same system so unresponsive to the desires of its workers and producers, desires expressed peacefully, legally and democratically, at the ballot box?

Have we reached a juncture where the validity of grievances is measured by the militancy of one's spokesman, and the decibel count of one's followers? Is it only the squeaky wheel that gets the grease, the hell-raisers who get their way in the modern democracy?

Back in the salad days of the children's crusade, Justice Douglas declared, "We must realize that today's establishment is the new George III. Whether it will continue to adhere to its tactics we do not know. If it does, the redress, honored in tradition, is also revolution."[2] From Kanawha County, West Virginia, to South Boston High in the cradle of liberty, some middle Americans, to whom "today's establishment" means "liberal establishment," seem prepared to take the Justice at his word.

Among conservatives, there is puzzlement and bitterness that, alone among the "movements" of the sixties, theirs seems barren of issue.

The civil rights movement can claim partial credit for the swiftest economic, political and social advance of any minority in history. Half a dozen pieces of landmark legislation have been enacted into law, half a dozen federal sub-agencies have been created, the charter of which is indistinguishable from that of the National Association for the Advancement of Colored People.

The environmentalists have had their movement institutionalized in the Environmental Protection Agency, the Council on Environmental Quality, and draconian federal laws for cleaner air and water. As for Mr. Nader and his consumer movement, they can count one federal agency born, Congress pregnant with another, and consumer counselors and allies in most every agency of the U.S. Government.

Even the women's liberation movement has nearly managed to have its own amendment grafted onto the Constitution, having succeeded in getting females, 51 percent of the nation, declared a "minority" for purposes of preferential hiring.

As for the anti-war movement, it unhorsed one President, contributed to the dissolution of the postwar foreign policy consensus on Communist containment, and helped turn America away from victory in Vietnam. And the peace movement can enter a valid claim for partial credit for the military and political disaster which followed in the spring of '75.

But what do conservatives have to show for their capture of the Republican Party in 1964, the nomination and election of Richard Nixon in 1968, the triumphs of Wallace, Nixon and Agnew in 1972? What endures—other than Burger, Blackmun, Rehnquist and Powell?

After a decade of primary, convention and electoral triumphs, capped by the landslide of '72, it can fairly be said of what we have wrought, what was said of the empire of Ozymandias:

> Nothing beside remains. Round the decay
> Of that colossal wreck, boundless and bare
> The lone and level sands stretch far away.

Why is this so? Why, for example, did not the Republican Administration seize the opportunity presented by the anti-Great Society votes of Nixon and Wallace, by terminating the liberal programs and turning the nation rightward in domestic and social policy?

Part of the answer lies in the social crisis of 1968, the President-elect's prognosis of the national condition and the necessary therapy and treatment.

Richard Nixon was elected in 1968 with the smallest fraction of the national vote since Woodrow Wilson in 1912. Not since Zachery Taylor in 1849 had a newly elected first-term President taken office with the opposition controlling both Houses of Congress. Beyond that the enormous bureaucracy in Washington was a sullen army more loyal to the Democrats who created it than the Republicans who inherited it. The Supreme Court was yet controlled by the Warren wing; and within the academic and journalistic communities, Richard Nixon was reviled as no other post-war politician with the single exception of the late Joseph McCarthy of Wisconsin.

Confronting this phalanx, the President believed that if stalemate was not to ensue, if he was to succeed in his declared endeavor to "bring us together," the first major gesture of compromise should come from the victors of '68. As it was foreign policy where the President's expertise and interest lay, it was domestic policy where he made the strategic concessions. Seeking to build a small reservoir of goodwill with a liberal establishment where a desert existed, he forewent the victor's prerogative of purging the bureaucracy. He declined to defund the Great Society.

The decision was not uncalculated. If his war policies would inflame the campuses, his domestic spending would at least cool the cities.

A "progressive" domestic policy held other attractions. As the China announcement, the appointment of John Connally and the reversal on wage-and-price controls demonstrated, Richard Nixon was ever a believer in the masterstroke.

Less a conservative than a fellow traveler of the right, Richard Nixon always held, with the late Senator Ashurst, that the clammy hand of consistency should never rest for long upon the shoulder of a statesman. He was less attracted by a reputation for orthodoxy than by the historic possibilities of "catching the Whigs swimming and stealing off with their clothes." And the newly installed President was not an inattentive student to the engaging Dr. Moynihan who would weave wonderful stories about a "new Disraeli" who would "dish the Whigs." Such stories produced greater pleasure than reading in his news summary yet another editorial attack on "the old Nixon."

And, so, the President made a conscious decision to shift leftward on domestic and social policy—to appease those who most opposed him. And the inexorable growth of the federal budget is a consequence of that decision.

Soon, the Nixon White House, elected to office on conservative oratory, was busy expropriating liberal slogans. We

are ourselves imposing "new priorities" on the budget, we asserted. Notice how defense spending is falling as a percentage
of federal spending and the GNP; notice how "spending for
human resources" is at record levels, relatively and absolutely.

Frustrated by the deadlock between the conservative
Arthur Burns and Patrick Moynihan, the President shifted
the domestic franchise to John Ehrlichman. Ex-advancemen,
managers and technicians were installed in the Domestic
Council. With the rise of the "pragmatists" in the White
House came victory, by default, for the liberals. For the in-
experienced technicians of John Ehrlichman were, like their
chief, less interested in the daily, bitter and bruising confron-
tations with the bureaucracy and press—which a conservative
domestic policy necessarily entails—than in winning plaudits
as "progressives" with "bold new programs" of their own.

Richard Whalen, the angry ex-aide to Mr. Nixon who
knows Washington well observed that when the Republicans
were elected in November of 1968, the bureaucracy was ter-
rified. By April and May of 1969, however, they were laugh-
ing again, secure once more in their programs, positions and
power, confident the new regime had no intention of disturb-
ing the old arrangements.

In 1968, the nation was prepared for conservative government at home; it voted for conservative government. We did
not provide that government. Not for four years did Mr.
Nixon draw the terrible swift sword on the bureaucracy or
the Great Society—and then it was too late. And the United
States is today paying for the lost opportunity—in economic
disorder, in a weakened currency, in a monstrous governmental establishment that threatens to consume half of the
national income, annually, by the year 2000. The opportunity
was ours to prevent this. We blew it—for a warehouse full of
press clippings.

In gratitude for his concessions all along the domestic front,
the liberals, within and without the Democratic Party, turned
loose the dogs of anti-war, who hounded the President's step
every foot of the way out of Southeast Asia. Nine months
after he asked Americans to go forward together, Mr. Nixon

and his Presidency were under siege. As they had done to Lyndon Johnson, his political enemies were on the verge—in Mr. Broder's phrase—of the "Breaking of the President." Contrary to the revisionist histories of the period, the Nixon Administration did not turn and confront its adversaries, until its policy of accommodation, concession and appeasement had visibly collapsed. In November of 1969, before Mr. Nixon went to the nation with the "great silent majority" speech, before Mr. Agnew embarked for Des Moines, to launch his "full retaliatory response" on the networks, the Administration was at Dunkirk.

In failing to purge the bureaucracy, immediately upon taking office, the President neglected the wise counsel of Machiavelli and of Macbeth, concerning political butchery:

> If it were done when 't is done, then
>   't were well
> It were done quickly

Had the President flushed the bureaucracy, and emasculated the Great Society in 1969, tens of billions of federal dollars would have gone unspent through 1974, and the nation never made to endure the double-digit inflation and consequent recession which have threatened the stability of the Republic.

Yet, the President's initial decision not to reflect his constituency and move rightward on social and economic policy in 1969 is only partial explanation why government fails to reflect the rightward drift in national sentiment. There are more enduring reasons, more intractable obstacles to a conservative counter-reformation.

Among these are the "special interests." During campaigns, candidates invariably concern themselves less with what the lobbyists are demanding or the editorial writers at *The New York Times* are saying than with what folks in the North Bronx are thinking. The demands of this or that interest group are less important than what the polls say people want to hear. So, during campaigns, candidates tend to move toward the right, nestling up alongside public opinion on such matters as federal deficits, marijuana, national defense and foreign aid. This was true in 1970, when one heard Senator Edward Kennedy suddenly equating campus commandos and Palestinian guerrillas. It was true in 1972 when Mr. McGovern, in the fall election, again and again, denied positions he had taken in the spring, with all the vehemence and indignation of Peter the Apostle in the courtyard of Caiphas. It was true in 1974 when Democrats expanded their congressional majority by deploring precisely the sort of spend-and-elect policies they had themselves practiced and would pursue again in the Ninety-fourth Congress.

Once an election is over, however, the broader constituency, the *vox populi*, falls silent. Then the voices of the special interests can be heard again in the land. Then, ideology again rears its head.

Safely reelected, Senator George McGovern in December flew out to his party's mini-convention in Kansas City, and delivered one of those Sons-of-the-Wild-Jackass speeches of his which would have bought him the farm politically, had he made it in Rapid City in October.

To most Americans, dependent upon the mass media, the term "special interest" conjures up visions of overwrought oil lobbyists lunging about the halls of Congress in defense of the depletion allowance or the Associated Milk Producers doling out campaign cash to purchase backing for a 5 percent hike in support prices.

But there are other "special interests," opposition to whose demands requires more courage and entails more risk than demagoging the oil industry. These are the immediate and direct beneficiaries of federal largesse—the 2,700,000 federal employees, the 5,600,000 getting unemployment benefits, the 11 million on welfare, the 20 million on food stamps, and the 31 million on social security—not to mention state and local government employees, teachers, veterans and the officers and enlisted men of the armed forces, increasingly dependent for their economic advancement upon the votes of the Congress of the United States. No congressional district is without thousands of these beneficiaries and their dependents. And a vote against a benefits increase or pay raise to one or more of such groups, many of them organized for political reprisal, can mean hundreds of volunteers marshaled for the defeat of the offending congressman.

In recent years, the explosion in federal spending has been led by increases in pay for federal employees, and direct "transfer payments" to individuals that in 1976 will run over $120 billion, consuming a third of the U.S. Budget, far more than Defense.

Almost 50 million Americans are now getting regular checks from Washington. Unless the inexorable rise in pay and benefits for these tens of millions is brought under control, unless politicians can resist the pressures these groups bring to bear, there is no hope of bringing the budget under control, no hope of significant tax relief for the productive private sector, no hope of bringing price stability back to where it was in the last days of Dwight Eisenhower, and the first days of John Kennedy.

The fiscal disaster of New York City, projected on a national scale, is what beckons if the United States government continues along the road it is traveling today at headlong speed, in fiscal year 1976.

A second obstacle is the national press. Not the Democratic Party, but the media is the first line of defense for American liberals, preventing an accurate translation of conservative sentiment in the country into conservative policy in the capital.

Almost every scrap of information Americans receive of their national government, its programs, policies and personalities, is filtered first through the distorting lens of the national press.

These individuals dictate which politicians will be presented to the country, and in what light they shall be perceived. They determine what issues shall be brought up for discussion in the forum of opinion, and what shall be the acceptable range of solutions offered. They control the forum of debate over public policy as absolutely as Speakers Tom Reed and Uncle Joe Cannon controlled the House. The media draws up the agenda of the nation's business; it determines who shall use the national microphones, and for how long. It is the ever-present moderator of the national debate; and it exerts a mighty influence upon the outcome.

This national press has become the gravedigger of our political parties. No state or national committee, no party contributors, can hope to offer incumbents, for fidelity to platform or principles, anything matching the rewards in publicity the big media provides those who break from the party ranks.

The media has major benefits to confer. And it confers them not upon the legislators who shape the great compromises, not on those skilled in parliamentary procedure, or effective in committee where the work is done. Rather the camera passes over movers and shakers like Congresswoman Edith Green of Oregon and Senator James Allen of Alabama to zero in on noisy and inconsequential dissenters like Bella Abzug and Charles Goodell.

It is the national press which, between elections, provides the daily pressure upon politicians to keep policy moving leftward. It is the big media which serves as publicity arm for the movements of liberalism and the left—i.e., civil rights, consumerists, environmentalists, women liberationists—at the expense of the concerns and issues raised by the right.

It is the national press, not the Democratic Party, which makes the case before the country for keeping OEO and Legal Services, for expanding not contracting food stamps, for a more conciliatory approach toward Castro, and a tougher policy toward South Africa and South Korea.

Beyond the big media, two other institutions loom large in the path of any President seeking to implement a conservative mandate at the ballot box. They are the federal bureaucracy and the federal courts. Much has been written about how the Imperial President usurped the powers of the Congress of the United States. But it is to the judiciary and the bureaucracy that Congress has truly surrendered authority and position.

These are the institutions which interpret and administer the laws with increasing indifference to congressional intent.

Judges and Justices appointed for life have become the final arbiters in social and political quarrels from abortion to the death penalty, from environmental regulations to welfare requirements, from the level of educational expenditures to the racial composition of classrooms. Political activists and reformers have gotten the message. More and more they by-pass legislatures and Congress and take their social and political causes into the courts, where the decisions are quicker and more certain.

Not simply the laws of Congress but the Constitution has been seized upon as a convenient vehicle by an impatient judiciary anxious to impose upon society its version of wise social policy and correct political theory.

In the sixties, the Warren Court "interpreted" the forefathers' dictum that government should be neutral between religions to mean that government should prefer non-religion. So prayer and the Bible are outlawed from the public schools of a nation whose most basic documents affirm a religious faith.

The same court construed "freedom of the press" to mean we are powerless to prevent pornographers from making every American city a rival of Copenhagen. The Fifth Amendment protection against self-incrimination, designed to prevent confessions extracted by force, has been stretched to create such a maze about the rights of criminals that the ends of the criminal justice system—prosecution of the guilty and protection of society—are almost lost. "Equal protection of the laws" was extracted from the Fourteenth Amendment and used as grounds for upholding executive action discriminating against white males.

The Bill of Rights might not win a majority vote in the United States, the civil libertarians weep. Well, whose fault is that? Is it not the fault largely of judicial ideologues who have perverted the Bill of Rights to impose upon the American people social policies they abhor, and in whose shaping they have had no voice?

What kind of government will we have, a lady inquired of the founding father emerging from the Constitutional Convention. "A republic, if you can keep it," replied Dr. Franklin. Less and less is ours a democratic republic. More and more are we governed by an unelected oligarchy of bureaucrats, judges and press, guided by their own ideology and insulated from the electorate and the common man.

As George Will has observed, "As the modern state grows, appointed officials increase in number and importance, while elected officials remain static in number and decline in importance."[3]

Why, other than inertia, does the bureaucracy resist the conservative mandate expressed at the polls? For a basic reason: self-interest, and survival. It is the bureaucrats' benefits, salaries, authority, position and power that face attrition if the will of the American people expressed at the ballot box is carried out by the politicians. If there are no more guidelines to be drawn up, no more corporations to bully, no more school boards to harass, no more reports to require, how, then, do bureaucrats justify their continued existence, let alone their expanding budgets?

It was against an arrogant distant bureaucracy that millions voted when they voted for George Wallace in the spring and Richard Nixon and Spiro Agnew in the fall of '72. And when President Ford, on taking office, announced that decision-making power would now be restored from the White House to the Cabinet, i.e., back to the bureaucracy, the Mandate of 1972, suspended during the Watergate months, was repealed.

So it is: The political pressure of millions dependent upon federal checks and federal benefits, and the entrenched and unresponsive power of the media, the bureaucracy and the courts, taken together, prevent implementation of a conservative mandate in American political life. This is why, as polls and surveys show the nation moving to the right, the government continues to move to the left.

As the Dartmouth scholar Jeffrey Hart has written, "What we have been creating therefore is the political equivalent of the famous San Andreas fault, in California. As everyone knows, along this fault line one part of the California landscape is moving in one direction, while the rest of it moves in the opposite direction. Enormous stresses will result in some kind of geological convulsion. The geological convulsion expected from the San Andreas fault can be extended by analogy to American politics . . . Something has to give!"[4]

Herein lies the source of much of the tension in American life; herein the reason Wallace, paralyzed, remains the "relevant" figure in the Democratic Party. Herein lies the cause that millions are coming to consider participation in the democratic process, through the ballot box, like playing poker for matchsticks—an instructive exercise, perhaps, but one that bores readily, as it is devoid of meaning.

Central to that Niagara of tragedies that was Watergate is the lost opportunity to move against the political forces frustrating the expressed national will. In the winter of 1973, Richard Nixon had begun to move. The Administration had, in Jeffrey Hart's phrase, "joined the power issue with the media,"[5] all along the line. The omens were good that four more years would mean permanent rescue of the Supreme Court from the ideology of Brennan, Douglas and Marshall. A program was underway to seed the bureaucracy with technicians and politicians more loyal to the Mandate of '72 than the institutional appetites of HEW or HUD. The coalition the President and his men put together that November was truly the "new majority" for which conservatives for a decade had labored.

"I don't need both Houses of Congress for what I intend to do," the President told me after the election of 1972, "I will only need one-third of one House, plus one."

Then, James McCord took his letter to Judge Sirica.

As Irving Kristol wrote within weeks of the Watergate disclosures of the spring of '73:

> What is really important about Watergate is the discredit it has cast upon the pro-Nixon electoral coalition —or if you wish the anti-McGovern coalition—of 1972.

I do not think it is an exaggeration to say that it has broken the backbone of that coalition, and has terribly weakened the forces of political moderation in the United States.[6]

☆

Capitalism and the Intellectuals

I

Among the paradoxes of the age is that the most successful economic system of the 19th and 20th centuries is the least likely to survive, undisfigured, into the 21st. American capitalism is a fortress besieged.

Not because of manifest failure, or the superiority of competing systems. Despite the inflation and recession of the mid-seventies, Americans continue to enjoy the highest standard of living of any race of people in the history of mankind. Other nations, East and West, still measure themselves against an American yardstick, and speak of "catching up with the United States." Soviet Communism, principal antagonist of capitalism, testifies to its own inferiority with the high wall it maintains to keep out the consumer goods of the West, and with the clandestine concessions it negotiates to purchase the technology and machinery of the United States. Almost six decades after the Revolution to build the workers' paradise, the commissars for agriculture, to feed the Soviet populations, were making irregular runs on the corn and grain markets of the Middle West.

As for democratic socialism, the major industrial states

furthest along that road, Britain and Italy, are also the Western states closest to the precipice of economic ruin.

Among the less developed countries, it is the socialist regimes which are loudest and least sufferable in condemning capitalism's wickedness that are, invariably, first in line with the largest bowls at the international soup kitchen America has run for the Third World for decades.

No, the threat to capitalism does not come from superior systems, or even from Arab oil sheiks. It emanates from within. Nowhere is the nature of that threat better summarized than in the famous memorandum Supreme Court Justice Lewis Powell, then a practicing attorney, penned to the Chamber of Commerce in 1971. The opening paragraphs are quoted here:

> No thoughtful person can question that the American economic system is under broad attack . . . the assault . . . is broadly based and consistently pursued. It is gaining momentum and converts.
>
> The sources are varied and diffused. They include . . . the Communists, New Leftists and other revolutionaries who would destroy the entire system, both political and economic. These extremists of the left are far more numerous, better financed and increasingly are more welcomed and encouraged by other elements of society, than ever before in our history. But they remain a small minority and are not yet the principal cause for concern.
>
> The most disquieting voices joining the chorus of criticism come from perfectly respectable elements of society: from the college campus, the pulpit, the media, the intellectual and literary journals, the arts and sciences and from politicians. In most of these groups the movement against the system is participated in only by minorities. Yet, these often are the most articulate, the most vocal and the most prolific in their writing and speaking.
>
> Moreover, much of the media—for varying motives

and in varying degrees—either voluntarily accords unique publicity to these "attackers" or at least allows them to exploit the media for their purposes. This is especially true of television which now plays such a predominant role in shaping the thinking, attitudes and emotions of our people.[1]

That the "most vocal and the most prolific" men of words are leading the assault against capitalism, and its central figure, the businessman, is evident in politics and public opinion.

On the network news, rare is the appearance by the man of business, except when he is charged with polluting some stream, reaping "windfall profits," or being indicted for corruption.

Where are the plays and novels where the businessman is cast as a sympathetic figure? Where are the movies and television shows that portray the man of industry as protagonist or hero? The businessman is almost a refugee from the cultural life of his own nation.

The men of words have been conducting the assault against capitalism for generations. In the last decade, however, they have moved from strength to strength. As a consequence, the American corporation ranks among the least admired of our institutions; and surveys show a near unanimity of Americans wanting government to "crack down" harder upon business.

Consider two incidents. When President Nixon, in the wake of the post-Cambodia disorders, referred to students who "blow up campuses" as "bums," it was adjudged an act of unforgivable *lèse majesté* against a splendid and idealistic generation. When President John F. Kennedy, enraged over Big Steel's price hike, blurted: My father always told me that all businessmen were "sons-of-bitches," but I never believed him until now, there were nods and chuckles of understanding in the editorial offices of the metropolitan press.

Politicians have been quick to sense the growing disfavor in which business is held. Senator Henry Jackson, known in times past to genuflect on entering Mr. Meany's vestibule, now sounds for all the world, when discussing the oil companies, like a latter-day Ida Tarbell.

More and more is the animus against business reflected in legislation. Tougher environmental, health and safety standards are imposed willy-nilly on industry. New regulations for the conduct of business are regularly promulgated. And the corporate tax burden in this bastion of free enterprise remains among the highest in the industrial world. Bridled by regulation, saddled with an enormous tax load, American capitalism has begun to falter in creating jobs and sustaining our prosperity.

The struggle is not one in which the right can adopt the stance of disinterested neutral. For as economic freedom is related to political freedom, so, the businessman is first cousin to the conservative. If his end of the dinghy sinks, how long can ours stay afloat? The fate of capitalism and the fate of modern conservatism are joined. It is no coincidence that the passing of Britain as a great power, and the decline of the British nation proceeded, *pari passu*, with the rise of British socialism.

Both for the nation, whose place in the sun cannot be maintained without economic power, and for the conservative, there are few more crucial concerns than the successful defense of capitalism against the current assault. Any such defense requires an understanding of the adversary; and of the root causes of the conflict. They can be traced back for centuries.

II

It is among the axioms of politics that the residence of the intellectual is on the left. His congenital dissatisfaction with things as they are, his enthusiasm for change, even radical change, makes of the intellectual the natural antagonist of the conservative. Whether the issue is organized religion, patriotism, authority, the capitalist system or traditional values, the conservative customarily finds himself a defender, and the intellectual a critic, indeed, an adversary, of the system and society to which he belongs.

It was not always thus.

In ancient empires and medieval kingdoms the men of words were often among the most loyal of subjects. The epic poetry of Homer and Virgil mythologized the histories of Greece and Rome. In Elizabethan England, Shakespeare and the other poets and playwrights were, many of them, more royal than the queen, celebrating Protestant England over Catholic Spain.

The breach between the men of words, the *république des lettres*, and the state and society, seems to date to the eighteenth century, and to France. In his classic *Reflections on the Revolution in France*, Edmund Burke traced one of the tributaries back to its source:

> Since the decline of the life and greatness of Louis the XIVth, (men of letters) were not so much cultivated, either by him or by his regent, or the successors to the crown; nor were they engaged to the court by favours and emoluments so systematically as during the splendid period of that ostentatious and not impolitic reign.
>
> What they had lost in the old court protection, they endeavoured to make up by joining in a sort of incorporation of their own.
>
> The literary cabal has some years ago formed something like a regular plan for the destruction of the Christian religion. This object they pursued with a degree of zeal which hitherto had been discovered only in the propagators of some system of piety.[2]

With the death of the Sun King, the men of words, having lost their place at court, contends Burke, began, with their pens, to wage savage war against the Crown, and against the Church which sustained the Crown.

Belief in God, proclaimed Diderot, author of the *Encyclopédie*, is bound together with submission to autocracy. The two rise and fall together; "men will never be free till the last king is strangled with the entrails of the last priest." His contemporary, Voltaire, took to signing off his letters with the motto, "Écrasez l'infame,"—crush the infamy of the church.

Frederick the Great of Prussia knew how to cope with such fractious intellectuals. As he wrote a contemporary, when Voltaire, while at Frederick's court, had managed to involve himself in a Saxon bond scandal, "I shall want him at the most another year . . . one squeezes the orange and throws away the rind." Louis XVI, a less capable and decisive prince, listened to the intellectuals, made concession after concession, and paid with his head.[3]

In working, then, for the destruction of the Church and the overthrow of monarchies, the motivation of the men of words was not difficult to discern. Once the old institutions fell, when the new order was established, the men of words would replace the priests as the moral arbiters, and, unlike most of the clergy, their place in heaven would not be deferred until the next world. Not without motive has anti-Catholicism been called the anti-Semitism of the intellectuals. As Irving Kristol has noted of his colleagues, " . . . the intellectual, lacking in other-worldly interests, is committed to the pursuit of temporal status, temporal influence and temporal power with a single-minded passion that used to be found only in the highest reaches of the Catholic Church. Way back in 1797, Benjamin Constant observed that 'in the new society where the prestige of rank is destroyed, we—thinkers, writers, and philosophers—should be honored as the first among all citizens.' The only reason Constant did not say, 'we intellectuals' is that the term had not yet come into common usage."[4]

To overthrow the court, and replace the clergy, intellectuals were busy in the eighteenth, nineteenth and twentieth centuries mining the foundations of the dynasties of Europe from Paris to St. Petersburg. Yet, the question arises: Why did the constitutional republics and parliamentary democracies, which succeeded the absolute monarchs, never regain the sustained allegiance or political enthusiasm of the men of words?

Even as democracy continued its upward march, as the freedoms of the common man expanded, as the material well-being of the working class improved in the nineteenth and twentieth centuries, still the intellectuals seethed with resentment at the society around them.

A quarter century before the French Revolution, Rousseau had written, "Man is born free, and everywhere he is in chains." Six decades after that pivot point in world history, Marx was echoing Rousseau, "the proletarians have nothing to lose but their chains . . . workers of the world unite!"

The stance of the remembered artists and intellectuals of the era was that of social rebel and political belligerent. From Italy the English poet Shelley wrote, "I met murder on the way. He had a mask like Castlereagh," the British foreign minister. When Wordsworth, among the fathers of the English romantic movement, accepted the official title of Poet Laureate, Robert Browning reacted, as did his colleagues, with disgust, charging Wordsworth with breaking from the ranks of "freemen," and sinking "to the rear of the slaves."

> Just for a handful of silver he left us,
> Just for a riband to stick in his coat.

In the United States, the most successful of the democratic republics, artists and intellectuals have for decades considered an adversary stance toward society to be among their defining characteristics. From T. S. Eliot to the expatriates of Hemingway's generation, to James Baldwin and Gore Vidal, it is deemed essential by writers that they escape America and go abroad, before they can do creative work.

The reasons advanced by the intellectuals to explain their alienation are unconvincing. Some maintain that they can never be truly at home in a country where the bourgeois tastes of workers and middle class set the standard for society. Others profess themselves outraged by a society that tolerates injustices against the poor, the weak and the black. But, only a Utopian, who has wandered outside of history, can remain hostile on such grounds, when one considers what passes for social justice throughout the world.

No, the heart of the intellectual's quarrel with America is deeper, more fundamental, than that. His grievance is not that America has been unfair to its workers or blacks or poor, but that it has been unfair to him. His class, the intellectuals, is the minority whose rights, privileges and perquisites are his consummate concern.

Believing themselves the most cultured, intelligent, and able in society, intellectuals are bitter with America because she has never accorded them their rightful status as "first among all citizens."

In working for the overthrow of monarchies and churches, the men of words believed that, at last, they would come into their own. But even as the political revolutions were underway in Europe and the Americas, another revolution was just beginning. This revolution, the industrial revolution, also succeeded, and it brought in its van a new class, the capitalist and the businessman, who, in riches and rewards, replaced the old nobility. To the intellectual, it is the men of business who have usurped the positions that should have been reserved for him within the new society. It is the businessman, not the intellectual, who, in the modern industrial society, sits at the head of the table and carves.

As M. de Jouvenel observed a quarter of a century ago in his essay on the *Treatment of Capitalism by Intellectuals,*

> The intellectuals have been the major agents in the destruction of the ancient structure of Western society . . . but the new constitution of society puts a premium upon the "goods" which are most desired and brings to the forefront of society those who lead in the production of "goods." The intelligentsia has then lost to this "executive" class the primacy which it enjoyed when it stood as "the First Estate."[5]

This, he argues, helps explain why it is that "the intellectual community has waxed harsher in its judgment of the business community precisely while the business community was strikingly bettering the conditions of the masses, improving its own working ethics, and growing in civic consciousness."

For generations, the intellectuals have believed their intelligence has gone unrecognized, their talents unused, their superior moral worth unrewarded. How, indeed, are such men to render allegiance to a society and system where all the world beats a path to the door not of the man who writes the better poem, but the man who builds a "better mouse trap"?

III

Among the poor and oppressed of Europe, America has been looked upon for centuries as the land of freedom, opportunity, and hope. By the tens of millions, until the doors were shut in the twentieth century, immigrants poured into the United States. Today, thousands annually enter the country illegally, across our southern border with Mexico, to get at the economic opportunities offered to those who will work in the land of the Golden Door.

That uncritical enthusiasm and admiration for the United States, however, a hallmark of oppressed peoples, has never been a characteristic of the Western intellectual community. Indeed, from Paris to New Delhi, America has been the subject of such loathing and moral ferocity as has been visited upon no other nation outside of Hitler's Germany. The reasons are not distant.

Not only was this most successful of nations constructed with little assistance from the men of words, but the United States has, from its inception, been a land where the intellectual, worse than persecuted, has been ignored.

In the judgment of some, societies are measured not by the political freedom accorded the common man, or the living standards of the working class, but by the prestige and power conferred on the intellectual class. By these standards America has never measured up.

The enthusiasm of the intellectuals in this country for revolutions of the left, the sympathy supposedly intelligent men have showered indiscriminately on the experiments of terrorists and tyrants like Stalin and Mao, Ho Chi Minh and Castro, thus become understandable. As the longshoreman-philosopher, Eric Hoffer, has perceptively noted:

> In no other social order, past or present, has the intellectual so completely come into his own as in the Communist regimes. Never before has his superior status been so self-evident and his social usefulness so unquestioned. The bureaucracy which manages to control every field of activity is staffed by people who consider themselves intellectuals. Writers, poets, scientists, professors, journalists, and others engaged in intellectual pursuits are accorded the high status of superior civil servants. They are the aristocrats, the rich, the prominent, the indispensable, the pampered and petted. It is the wildest dream of the man of words come true.[6]

Under capitalism, however, it has not been intellectuals, but financiers, merchants, industrialists and businessmen to whom society long looked for leadership and guidance. Thus, the historic enmity of the men of words for the men of business. Envy is at the root of the current assault by intellectuals and their auxiliaries against the business community. And they have taken their revenge.

It was intellectuals who rewrote the history of the great era of capitalism and entitled it, "The Gilded Age." It was intellectuals who reshaped the image of the nineteenth-century "captains of industry," into "robber barons." It was intellectuals who helped fasten forever upon the industrialists of the First World War the label "merchants of death." It was intellectuals who applauded and assisted FDR in his campaign to drive "the moneychangers . . . from their high seats in the temple of our civilizations." And it is the modern liberal intellectual and his political auxiliaries Irving Kristol has in mind, when he writes: "The simple truth is that the professional classes of our modern bureaucratized societies are engaged in a class struggle with the business community for status and power."[7]

Whoever, here or abroad, declares himself an enemy of capitalism has the intellectuals for a friend. In the thirties, they lionized and romanticized the strikers of the labor movement. In the sixties, their affections and attentions were transferred to the environmentalists and the consumer movement. To Ralph Nader, they have played John the Baptist.

Prior to the New Deal, the ancient grudge borne toward men of business was of little concern to the latter, or the country. The number of intellectuals was small. Largely confined to the campuses, their influence was insignificant. The customary fashion in which the anti-capitalist professor gained his vengeance upon the businessman was to plant the seeds of radicalism in his children. Today, however, that has changed.

The numbers, influence and power of those who share, or sympathize with the intellectuals' views toward the nation's economic system, has grown exponentially. The reasons are at hand: mass education and the mass media.

Consider a few figures. In 1940, perhaps one in ten Americans were exposed to a college education; today it is two in five. Where perhaps a million and a half Americans were on campus in 1940, today the figure is 10 million. In 1940, only 186,500 bachelor degrees were awarded in the U.S.A.; in 1975, there were 950,000, and more than a million Americans were doing post-graduate work. For every Ph.D. graduated in 1940, 10 were graduated in 1970.

Though the value of the parchment has depreciated with the inflation of the currency, there are still hundreds of thousands, perhaps millions, who consider themselves "intellectuals," or who share the peculiar biases of that ethnic group. The "adversary culture," which some of them soaked up during their college years, they have taken with them into their careers.

More educated, more politically active than the average American, this new class does more than provide a market for the publications of the counter-culture, like the *New*

York Review of Books, and *Rolling Stone.* They have become dominant voices in publishing and the arts, in the academic community and the big foundations, in the public policy institutes, and the traditional media which is rapidly concurring in the verdict upon Big Business handed down long ago by the intellectual.

While the attitudes and attributes enumerated above do not apply to *all* intellectuals—there is a small but growing community of conservative and neo-conservative thinkers in America—they do apply to the majority of men and women who dominate the intellectual and cultural elite of this society. Within that community, there are perhaps some closet conservatives, but then there are also some political liberals in the NCO Club at Ft. Benning.

IV

The sea-change resulting from having introduced the millions to the adversary culture of the few was not unpredicted. In 1942, the great economist, Joseph Schumpeter, in his classic, *Capitalism, Socialism and Democracy,* peered across the decades and saw capitalism one day being brought low, by its very success.

Capitalism, the most successful of economic systems, would by its nature, argued Schumpeter, inevitably and steadily increase the wealth. As a consequence, the opportunity for higher education would open up for more and more young people. Having passed through colleges and universities, these young people would come to expect positions, status and influence commensurate with their heightened self-evaluation. As there are only so many such positions in any society, he contended, capitalism would be confronted with a "surplus of intellectuals." Because capitalism could not meet their demands for positions commensurate with their standing, these "intellectuals" would turn against the system.

Is that not what the United States confronts? There are five applicants for every teaching position in the departments of some major colleges. Young people, with advanced degrees, are being employed in what, for them, are "dead-end jobs," teaching in junior colleges or high schools, or even clerking at the supermarket or driving cabs.

Feeling cheated of the rewards that should be theirs by right of education, they provide a receptive audience for any attack upon "corporate greed." And when the intellectuals, with the support of this disgruntled army and its political allies, begin their final assault upon the citadel of capitalism, who will defend it? The workers?

No, contends Schumpeter. Even though the worker is the primary beneficiary of capitalism, as he is the exploited victim of communism, workers do not understand economics. They do not know precisely to what they should attribute their high standard of living. They focus more upon their wants than upon the relative prosperity which they have come to take for granted. Further, the worker will not defend capitalism because he has been taught by the men of words that the businessman is his enemy.

Thus we see workers and unions applauding political demands for higher taxes on the very corporate profits upon which their own jobs may depend. In Gary, Indiana, we see steelworkers siding with the Environmental Protection Agency against United States Steel when victory means the shutting down of a furnace and the loss of jobs.

But what of the businessman himself? Certainly, he is capable of defending the system which guarantees his own prosperity? No again, answers Schumpeter.

When the final assault upon capitalism comes, the first generation of entrepreneurs, the captains of industry, the men who created, *de novo*, the great commercial, industrial and financial empires will have passed on. Control of their empires will have passed to a new generation, the managers and technocrats, men who rose to their current station because of superior skill in negotiating the corporate ladder. Neither by temperament nor training will such company bureaucrats be capable of holding and defending what they inherited, contends Schumpeter—especially on the avenue of advance along which the attack will come, on the grounds of emotions and values.

Have not Schumpeter's predictions come to pass when we see, on national television, the lions of the oil industry bleating like so many shorn lambs before Henry Jackson and Abraham Ribicoff?

We can measure the distance we have traveled by considering how E. H. Harriman (not Averell, the son) and James J. Hill, the first Rockefeller and the first Ford, J. P. Morgan and Henry Clay Frick would have responded to the non-negotiable demands of a handful of hirsute environmentalists and consumer advocates.

For the ideological struggle in which he finds himself, few individuals are more poorly trained or ill-prepared than the modern executive. As Benjamin Rogge, professor of political economy at Wabash College observed a year ago, in his exegesis of Schumpeter's thesis:

> . . . the businessman lacks the capacity to capture the imagination of society . . . Listen to what Schumpeter says, "A genius in the business office may be, and often is, utterly unable outside of it to say boo to a goose, both in the drawing room and on the platform . . . Knowing this, he wants to be left alone and to leave politics alone. There is surely no trace of the mystic glamor about him which is what counts in the ruling of men. The stock exchange is a poor substitute for the Holy Grail." In effect, the businessman has no charisma and no sex appeal. Or as Stendhal put it, "Far be it from me to conclude that industrialists are not honorable. All I mean is that they are not heroic!"[8]

This, then, is the vulnerability of the man of business.

He is in business, quite simply, to make money. While it may be cogently demonstrated his pursuit of profit creates jobs, expands wealth, and guarantees the prosperity of us all, still, the pursuit of monetary gain is seen today as something unheroic, if not sordid. To the young, many of whom already know the sweetness of affluence, the corporate job offer cannot compete with the intellectuals' siren call to "improve the quality of life," to "remake America," to "establish social justice." No system in history has done more for the common man than capitalism, but the businessmen are intellectually incapable, as a class, of making the case.

If the workers will not defend the enterprise system, and the businessman cannot, is then capitalism an undefended fortress, certain to fall? So, it would seem.

What we are witnessing is the unfolding of the drama about which Schumpeter forewarned three decades ago. We have come 180 degrees from that place in our history where the entrepreneur was a man romanticized in literature, and admired and emulated by the young. Far from being considered a benefactor, the businessman, in some influential circles, is viewed as the principal threat to the quality of life. He is seen and portrayed as the embodiment of greed, fouling the air, polluting the waters, ravaging the natural beauty of the countryside, all to turn out useless and overpriced products to reap windfall profits for himself.

Meanwhile, the new intellectual class, fawned upon by the liberal press, has moved out of the academic community into the tax-exempt and tax-supported institutions, foundations, public policy research centers, public interest law firms and the expanding bureaucracies of state and federal government. The intellectuals' animosity toward business is being translated into public policy. The number of agencies and commissions designed to watch, regulate and control private enterprise—each more militant than its predecessor—continues to rise.

Indeed, the true feelings of the intellectuals toward business have come out of the classroom seminar; they are now respectable. On many campuses, an attack upon "corporate greed" or "obscene profits" is guaranteed thundering applause from faculty and students whose own institution may depend upon corporate profits, dividends or contributions. Some of the nation's most powerful media provide tens of millions in annual free publicity to political attacks on the very corporations upon whose advertising revenues the networks and metropolitan press depend for survival. Triumph after triumph of ideology over interest.

When the late Salvador Allende seized the copper mines of Anaconda, and the telephone properties of ITT, hardly a whimper of protest was heard from the academic community or the national press—even though taxpayers, or middle-class shareholders by the thousands, would have to make good the loss. Their rage and indignation were reserved for our own Government when it used its leverage in the financial markets —and deployed the CIA—in retaliation against the thieves of Santiago.

V

As anticipated, the businessman's response to the attack upon his motives and achievements has been feeble and ineffectual. He has paid out huge lecture fees to have his most hostile critics appear before business gatherings, "so we may better understand what they are trying to say." He has publicly confessed his sins, and made a firm purpose of atonement. He has pledged to "continue the dialogue." He has used tens of millions of dollars to purchase ads on the very stations and in the selfsame publications where his adversaries are given the run of the news columns and the airwaves. He has expanded his P. R. department, beefed up the Washington lobbying operation, and gone back to work.

As Kevin Phillips has written, contemptuously, of the big oil companies under fire, ". . . millions have been given to public broadcasting, orchestras, community action groups and the like, while other large sums have been poured into full-page color advertising (read 'subsidies') in chic liberal magazines. To some extent the international oil companies are paying off the liberals and leaving conservatives holding the bag."[9]

Businessmen need to understand that they cannot bribe their way out of the crisis of capitalism. They cannot buy their way into the good graces of ideologues by contributing to the symphony or buying a table of tickets to the Corcoran Ball. Ralph Nader will still be there, making his accusations and demands, long after the Corvair no longer capsizes, cornering at 28 miles-an-hour, long after every car on an American highway has a catalytic converter and air bag.

What Nader and his allies seek is not reform, but power. They are social revolutionaries. They want a new economic system where final decision-making authority over the nation's business and industry no longer resides with the corporate officers or boards of directors, but in Washington, where Mr. Nader and his allies can influence or make those decisions themselves. The consumer movement—like other liberal "crusades" of our era—is a popular front of reformers, liberals and ideologues, the latter of whom are exploiting consumer dissatisfaction to advance their own political objectives and careers.

These were the individuals Hamilton had in mind when he warned in the Federalist Papers of that "dangerous ambition," which "lurks behind the specious mask of zeal for the rights of the people."

In the economic crisis of the middle seventies, these men see opportunity. Should business, hobbled by taxes and regulation, fail to pull the nation out of the ditch into which the policies of government have plunged it, they will not be disappointed. The chorus will then go up for government to "rescue the people from the consequences of corporate greed."

We are not far away from outright demands for nationalizing industry when William Raspberry, columnist for *The Washington Post*, can write casually, "Holman and I pondered the insanity of having four-fifths of the American economy in private hands, which is to say subject to the whims of businessmen whose guiding thought is maximum profit—even if it does harm to the nation as a whole."[10]

When one reflects upon conditions in those societies where government controls four-fifths of the economy, and government devotes itself to the material and moral uplift of the people, it is not difficult to conclude with Dr. Johnson that "a man is never more innocently involved than in the making of money."

VI

Despite the reversals of capitalism, the outcome of the conflict is not a foregone conclusion. Success, however, requires of the businessman that he recognize the nature of his adversary, and muster the courage and will to confront him, politically. As Justice Powell urged, "Business must learn the lesson long ago learned by labor and other self-interest groups. This is the lesson that political power is necessary; that such power must assiduously be cultivated, and that, when necessary, it must be used aggressively and with determination—without embarrassment and without the reluctance which has been so characteristic of American business."[11] Mr. Meany and Mr. Barkan are not loved; they are respected.

Despite the seeming inevitability of their triumph, the liberal establishment is not invincible; it is soft at the core. Intellectuals have no hold on the political allegiance of the working or middle class. Much of the esteem in which academics were once held was erased by their squalid performance when confronted by the militants of the student left in the last decade. And while liberal intellectuals fashion themselves the benefactors of the working class, it is the working class, dirt farmers and factory hands, who come to their feet cheering and stomping, when George Wallace takes off after the "pointy-headed pseudo-intellectuals who can't park a bicycle straight."

The preferred politics of the intellectual are the politics of the elite. Almost half of McGovern's delegates had done postgraduate work, reflective of only a tiny minority of Americans. On issues from gun control to abortion, amnesty to marijuana, welfare to national defense, businessmen have more in common with their employees and workers than does the intellectual.

As Herman Khan has noted, there is a great gulf in America between the upper middle class "progressives" and the average citizen. "The upper middle class, the group running the media, the educators, city planners, some students—all are basically out of touch with reality. It is a very specific illness of a very specific group, less than ten percent of the country."[12]

If businessmen can be charged with having profit as their highest goal, then the intellectual can be charged with seeking power as his divinity. This, indeed, is the "dirty little secret" of liberalism. Behind all the talk about "social justice," "equality" and "strengthening the public sector" lies the inexorable drive for power.

The intellectuals prefer the public to the private sector, the state to the corporation, because when wealth, power and resources are shifted from the private sector to government, they are transferred from institutions where liberals and intellectuals are ignored, to a bureaucracy where liberals and intellectuals reign supreme.

For ten years we have heard from the academic community, echoed in the media, the demand for "new priorities" in federal spending. Those priorities have been imposed upon the budget—and *cui bono?* To whose benefit? Budgets for weapons, agriculture and space have dropped relatively and absolutely. Meanwhile, budgets for education, social programs, arts, humanities, community action, legal services have all risen geometrically. A cornucopia of jobs, consultancies and special assistantships has opened up for the intellectuals who have poured into the bureaucracy, where the salary scales have risen far more rapidly than pay in the private sector.

Despite political victories by the right in primaries, conventions and national elections, the last ten years have been the salad days of liberalism. The machinery of government is now in place and working assiduously for the benefit of its operators.

The Brookings Institution, policy institute of the left, works hand-in-glove with bureaucrats and Democrats to devise still newer social programs, the successful implementation of which will require the hiring of still more Brookings scholars.

Once a political philosophy, liberalism hardened into an ideology, and has now become big business, and is becoming a racket. That the status, position and authority of the intellectuals has risen so in recent years is no accident. It was designed that way. The Leviathan welfare state over which a handful of Republicans temporarily preside is a wonder of the modern world, a pyramid to ambition masquerading as altruism.

VII

What can the businessman do? A great deal, if he will use in his own defense his position and his discretionary power over corporate funds. Businessmen sit upon the boards of trustees of most of the nation's private colleges. They are the alumni who make the large annual donations. They should link future contributions to a non-negotiable demand that capitalism be given due process in the department of economics, that the role of the businessman in American life be given fair treatment in the department of history. In the local school system, they should make a similar demand. Blacks, women, labor, native Americans, every interest group in the country has demanded that textbooks not exclude their special contribution in the nation's history. Private enterprise, which built twentieth-century America, should go forth and do likewise.

Secondly, big business should establish a monitoring system of the nation's networks. Whenever the business point of view in a controversy is distorted or ignored, a complaint should be filed with the FCC. Should any network continually discriminate in its news programs in favor of consumerists or environmentalists, against business, then as large a share of business' advertising budget as possible should be withdrawn from the network. The withdrawal of advertising will hurt business some, but it will hurt the networks more—and will bring the latter to a sudden realization that Big Business is no longer the paper tiger of American politics.

Nemo me impune lacessit, that splendid motto of the Scots, is one that businessmen, like their predecessors of a century ago, should adopt. If West Virginia coal miners are willing to suffer hardships out on strike for a few more dollars in wages, then businessmen should make commensurate sacrifices to defend the system which benefits them, and us all.

The situation that exists today, from the standpoint of capitalism, is worse than scandalous; it is, in Edith Efron's term, "suicidal." "The antagonism to capitalism of the nation's airwaves . . . is a hard cultural fact," she argues; this "communications assault on the freedom of the American businessman" is being financed by the American businessman. "Without the money from Big Business, no such nation-wide assault could take place . . . U.S. capitalism is systematically financing its own destroyers."[13] It ought to stop.

Further, businessmen should use their discretionary capital to buy media, and turn it around. As Arthur Schlesinger has correctly observed, power—which in Marxian terms meant control of the means of production—in the modern world means control of the means of communication.

Today, political liberals who share the *Weltanschauung* of the intellectual elite control the national press and the networks. They dispatch their muckrakers and investigators to expose the alleged power, arrogance, corruption and abuses of institutions high on *their* enemies list: the Pentagon, the FBI, the CIA and Big Business. Meanwhile, institutions dominated by political liberals, such as the welfare state, the Ford Foundation and its satellites, the academic community and especially the national press itself, are exempt from the kind of searching inquiry to which conservative institutions are regularly subject.

Businessmen should use their wealth to reward their supporters and punish their adversaries. Newspapers, magazines, colleges, public policy institutes that traditionally or consistently show an anti-business bias should be cut off without a dime. And those publications and institutions which support the system that enables business to prosper should be supported in turn.

The businessman is engaged in a class war with upper-middle-income liberals for authority and social position. Nothing would advance his cause more than to abandon this struthious posture of benign neutrality, for one of active belligerency. At the next tax reform hearings, the men of business should be there not only to defend their position, but to attack the loopholes of the left, the big foundations, and to demand and know why it is that corporate taxes are going to subsidize tax-free public policy institutes and "public interest law firms" which use their privileged positions as a base from which to launch assaults upon business.

The businessman should borrow the intellectuals' dog-eared copy of the Murray Chotiner handbook of American politics, the first chapter of which opens: stay on the attack. Businessmen should cease spending their waking hours defending their existence, and begin demanding to know what other institutions are contributing. Are the universities so successful in educating the young that college professors are in a position to criticize others? Or is it true, as Jeffrey Hart writes, that it is no coincidence that universities, the only institutions run entirely by intellectuals and liberals, are also those institutions furthest along the road toward disintegration?

Have the politicians managed the economy so brilliantly that senators and congressmen are in positions to make judgments about business prices and profits? Is not Mr. Ralph Nader's consumer protection agency every bit as much a hunk of pork barrel for consumer advocates, in line for the prime jobs, as is an increase in milk support prices for dairy farmers?

But the businessman cannot win unless he recognizes he is in a fight, a political and ideological conflict. And his refusal to participate does not mean the struggle ends, but that he will lose and the rest of us with him.

☆

On Integration and Education

I

With the lone exception of Lyndon Johnson's, no Administration so consciously tilted policy toward black America as did Richard Nixon's.

Carl Rowan and the Black Caucus may not leave that statement undisputed. Yet, it contains more truth than error. Though Mr. Nixon's government shorted the civil rights community on rhetoric, it was not short on delivery. And though John Newton Mitchell does not seem destined to become a revered figure in black America, there was truth as well as irony in his retort, "Watch what we do, not what we say."

Consider. In Mr. Nixon's first four years:

· The civil rights enforcement budget rose 800 percent to more than $600 million.

· Record numbers of blacks were appointed to federal posts. In executive positions, with salaries above $20,000, there was an increase of 37 percent. The day the President resigned, blacks, who constitute 10 or 11 percent of the population, held 16 percent of all federal jobs.

· The "Philadelphia Plan," forcing open union training programs and job lists was devised and imposed. Quotas for black academicians, poorly disguised as "goals and timetables," were imposed upon college and university faculties.

· In fulfillment of the candidate's 1968 commitment to "black capitalism," the Office of Minority Business Enterprise was created, and funded to the level of $63 million a year.

· Federal purchases from minority enterprises rose from $9 million to $153 million.

· Small business loans to minorities increased over 1,000 percent from $41 million to $435 million.

· U.S. aid to black colleges more than doubled.

· U.S. deposits in minority-owned banks rose from $2 million to $80 million.

· More school integration was achieved in four years than in the previous fifteen since *Brown v. Board of Education*, without violence, and without troops. "It has been only since 1968 that substantial reduction of racial segregation has taken place in the South," declared the U.S. Commission on Civil Rights in March of 1975.[1]

· Food-stamp recipients, among whom are many poor and working-class blacks, rose from 2.5 million to 11 million in 1972 and 15 million in mid-1974.

· Welfare rolls doubled from 5.3 to 10.9 million. And Richard Nixon introduced the first "guaranteed income" any President proposed to an American Congress. What he recommended in 1969 was that the Reverend Ralph David Abernathy and the denizens of Resurrection City were shouting about in 1968.

True, the former President's civil rights record was not unblemished. With the thunder rolling on the right, Mr. Nixon's enthusiasm for H.R. 1, the Family Assistance Plan, waned and finally evaporated. The President's men were also something less than subtle in airing their opposition to forced bussing. And the White House had to be dragooned into endorsement of a five-year extension of the Voting Rights Act of 1965. Though endorse it we did.

On balance, however, Richard Nixon's record on behalf of

black America is infinitely more impressive than that, say, of John F. Kennedy, who dithered for nearly two years before he could pick up a pen and sign the executive order outlawing discrimination in federally subsidized housing.

Yet the national portrait of John F. Kennedy hangs in a place of honor in the homes of civil rights leaders who, even at the height of Mr. Nixon's popularity, would have happily hanged him in effigy. Why?

The Kennedy cult stems largely from the tragic circumstances of the late President's death. But, even before his assassination, John F. Kennedy had earned the allegiance of blacks not through benefaction or legislation like Lyndon Johnson but through exploitation of the dramatic gesture. The phone call to Mrs. Martin Luther King during the 1960 campaign, the dispatch of marshals and troops to the campus at Oxford, Mississippi, the commissioning of Mr. Katzenbach to confront George Wallace in the school house door—all were the stuff of high drama at which the late President excelled.

In terms of achievement, however, what? One black going to classes at Ole Miss, and 1.2 percent of blacks in the South in desegregated schools, almost a decade after Brown.

But what the Kennedys knew instinctively, however, is what Republicans rarely learn. As JFK showed with his eloquent and empty bravado in Miami about the flags of the Bay of Pigs brigade one day flying again in a free Havana, with some constituencies, the symbolic gesture of solidarity has infinitely greater meaning than any legislative accomplishment.

Still, the question lingers. Why, considering the record, was it only among blacks that Richard Nixon registered no gains between the cliff-hanger of '68 and the avalanche of '72? Nearly 90 percent voted against him in both elections. Why did civil rights leaders, who knew the full record, speak of him as an enemy of the race.

If Richard Nixon had shifted position between 1960, when he ran so well among blacks, and 1972 when he ran so poorly, it was to move leftward on civil rights.

Part of the answer lies in the changed·character of the civil rights leadership itself. In the sixties, the nation's black political leadership moved from victory to victory. It was courted, coddled and fawned upon by the press as no other assemblage of politicians in history. Even today, it is kowtowed to by the Democratic Party in a manner approaching the servile. When the terrifying threat swept the floor of the Kansas City mini-convention that, "Willie will walk," meaning Willie Brown and some blacks would walk out if they did not get their way, the party of Jefferson, Jackson, Roosevelt and Kennedy crumbled like a castle of sand.

For a decade no major political faction, left, right or center, has dared confront the civil rights community, regardless of how extreme its rhetoric or outrageous its demands.

Civil rights politicians have come to view themselves as the moral superiors of every other politician in the country. Theirs is the divine dictum that he who is not with me is against me. Their own is viewed as the only position consonant with moral rectitude. Opponents are not simply wrongheaded, but benighted, bigoted and racist at heart. The ossified leadership of the movement demands an undeviating loyalty to party line less characteristic of pressure groups in a democracy than of the militant wing of the Chinese Communist Party. Heroes of the civil rights movement, men who bear the scars of its great battle, are branded sell-outs for hedging a few centimeters on such an explosive question as forced bussing. The god of the civil rights movement is indeed a jealous god.

For conservatives, the lesson of the Nixon years seems cold, and clear. With such True Believers, who savage the most faithful of servants for a single indiscretion, no hope exists of fruitful collaboration.

Men of the right were long ago dismissed as racists. There exists no reason why they should not, openly and unapologetically, champion public opposition to the "second generation" of civil rights demands. For these demands, still coming in, cannot be met without unacceptable losses in freedom, without the use of methods abhorrent to a democracy.

The old generation of civil rights leaders sought an end to state-dictated discrimination in the public schools; the new demand is for state-dictated racial balance. The old wanted an end to discrimination in the sale and rental of housing; the new demand is that taxpayers subsidize housing for poor blacks in the heart of suburban white communities. The old generation wanted "color" eliminated as an arbitrary and unjust criterion for hiring and promotion; the new demand is that color be the principal criterion. "Equal rights" has been replaced by the demand for "equal rewards." Freedom, the battle cry of the old civil rights community, has given way to coercion.

Indeed, the term "civil rights," the battle cry of a movement which had justice on its side, is a misnomer for what is being demanded and done. It has become an umbrella slogan to cover up the demands of political profiteers and demagogues for a larger slice of federal boodle for themselves, and an officially sanctioned policy of reverse discrimination which would put blacks in the same preferred racial position whites enjoyed decades ago.

II

To view the radical change in the character of the demands, one need only return to the original goal of *Brown v. the Board of Education*, twenty-one years ago.

On December 9, 1952, arguing *Briggs v. Elliott* before the Supreme Court—one of five cases folded into the historic Brown decision of 17 May, 1954—NAACP Attorney, Thurgood Marshall, outlined his objective:

> . . . we are not asking for affirmative relief. That will not put anybody in any school. *The only thing that we ask for is that the State-imposed racial segregation be taken off,* and to leave the county school board, the county people, the district people, to work out their own

solution of the problem to assign children on any reasonable basis they want to assign them on. (Emphasis
added)

That this was precisely what the Court granted is evident
in the language of Chief Judge John Parker, in the 1955 decision on *Briggs v. Elliott,* on remand:

> The Constitution in other words does not require inte-
> gration. It merely forbids discrimination. It does not
> forbid such segregation as occurs as the result of volun-
> tary action. It merely forbids the use of governmental
> power to enforce segregation. The Fourteenth Amend-
> ment is a limitation upon the exercise of power by the
> state or state agencies, not a limitation upon the freedom
> of individuals . . .
> Nothing in the Constitution or in the decision of the
> Supreme Court takes away from the people freedom to
> choose the schools they attend.

For a dozen years this was the law of the land. The famous
1964 Civil Rights Act, rammed through Congress by President Lyndon Johnson, on a wave of national sentiment following the march on Washington in August of '63 and the
assassination of President Kennedy in November, specifically
prohibited children from being assigned to particular schools
"in order to overcome racial imbalance." In 1965, Congress
reaffirmed this directive, forbidding "any department, agency,
officer or employee of the United States to exercise any direction, supervision, or control over the personnel of any school
system . . . or to require the assignment or transportation of
students or teachers in order to overcome racial imbalance."
As columnist James J. Kilpatrick wrote, "that is plain language. Any child can comprehend it."[2]
But the Warren Court, impatiently watching as the sands
of its hourglass were running out, was uninterested in any intent of Congress. It had intentions of its own. Striking down
state and local laws as unconstitutional had not achieved the

racial integration the Court and its liberal allies had hoped. So, what had not come about by free choice, they sought to achieve by court decree.

In 1968, in *Charles C. Green v. County School Board of New Kent County, Virginia*, the Supreme Court threw out a valid, functioning freedom-of-choice plan, because the free choices of parents had resulted in decisions unsatisfactory to the Justices of the United States; and the Court mandated integration.

With the Green decision, the federal courts became as much dictators of the racial composition of classrooms as had the old segregationist states of the South. The iron rule of the segregationist was overthrown in 1954; in 1968, began the iron rule of the integrationist. It is no less tyrannical.

The evil against which the old civil rights leaders fought was having black children bussed 10 and 20 miles from home, because of the color of their skin. The relief they now seek is to have white children bussed 10 and 20 miles because of the color of *their* skins. The rationale: Presumably, black children perfectly capable of learning themselves the fundamentals of basketball, politics and music are incapable of learning the fundamentals of spelling and mathematics unless a contingent of white children have been imported to sit in the same classroom.

The Green decision stood Brown on its head. It made of school children precisely what the Court, in *Pierce v. the Society of Sisters*, had said they were not, i.e., "mere creatures of the State."

Even the politically moderate *Washington Star* seemed stunned by Green. "Federal judges," it editorialized, "have a constitutional duty and the competence to strike down any law which imposes school segregation. They have neither the duty nor the competence to demand compulsory integration and to run the schools by judicial fiat. The sooner the judges recognize this, the better it will be for our system of public education."[3]

But, the judges have not recognized this. They have not acknowledged any lack of competence to dictate to the

schools; and public education has suffered mightily as a consequence.

III

Anyone raised in the Washington community in the fifties
had an opportunity to witness first-hand the impact of ideology upon education. When the Chief Justice delivered the
Brown decision, in May of 1954, the author was a sophomore
in an inner-city Jesuit prep school. From our standpoint the
decision was welcome. No longer did we have to travel five
hours, one-way, by bus, into the Pennsylvania countryside to
towns like Conshohocken and Hershey to find a public high
school amenable to playing football with a Catholic team with
a black on the bench.

Riding to school, however, it was impossible not to notice
the "for sale" signs, marching block by block, week by week,
outward from the city until they reached suburban Silver
Spring, Maryland. Liberal, Democratic Washington, having
rejoiced in the Court's decision, was fleeing to the suburbs.
The entire process from *de jure* segregation to integration to
de facto resegregation of the D.C. public schools, required
only a few years. Today, the Washington public school system is 96 percent black.

Egalitarianism was the reigning passion of those years, and
these; and it was not without its cost for education.

Where Gonzaga High School was just off First and I
Streets, N.W., down the street at First and N was Dunbar,
then the most famous black high school in the United States.
Eighty percent of Dunbar students, highest in the metropolitan area among public and private schools, went on to college.
Military training was mandatory; discipline was excellent;
the courses were wholly academic; the curriculum as advanced as any in the city. Among Dunbar's graduates are the
first black Senator since Reconstruction, the first black to
serve in the Cabinet, the first black General in the United
States Army.

The entire black community took pride in Dunbar High.

Students applied there from all over the country. What blacks had in Dunbar, Catholics had in Gonzaga and Georgetown Prep, and the city's establishment had in St. Alban's and Landon—a high school of genuine academic exellence.

Swept up by the fever of "equality," following the Supreme Court decision, however, D.C. school officials abolished Dunbar as a quality academic institution, and turned it into another neighborhood school. Located in one of the poorer sections of Washington, it today ranks, academically, near the bottom of D.C. public schools, themselves below the national norm.

A dozen years later, Federal Judge J. Skelly Wright, took the new egalitarianism a step further. Not only were there to be no superior high schools within the system, there were no longer to be superior classes within the high schools. The "track system" which segregated children, not by race, but by learning capacity—so that each could be taught according to his ability—was abolished. The brightest and the dullest were taught at the same pace.

Only one step remains for the courageous court that dictates to the D.C. schools; to outlaw discrimination by coaches in inter-high athletics against students who are slower, weaker and shorter than the varsity football and basketball teams.

Ideology has been served, but has the community? Most of the white children with academic talent—whose parents could afford to move out of the city—have left the D.C. public schools. Many black children, who stayed in the D.C. schools, have been robbed of the learning experience they might have had—had Judge Wright not forced them into classrooms where the pace of education was geared to the dullest.

Not only in Washington, but across the country, judges and bureaucrats and educational ideologues have been creating the kind of public schools they would never dream of forcing their own children to attend. Black America, which depends most on these schools, has paid the price.

Nor does one need a multi-million dollar study by the National Institute of Education to know what is necessary to restore quality to the schools, and confidence in the system. All one need do is examine the difference between the parochial schools, which parents will pay hundreds of dollars a year to have their children attend, and the public schools, which parents will pay thousands to have their children avoid. Why was Dunbar such an enormous success with not a third of the budget of the average D.C. high school today?

The sooner judges, bureaucrats and educational ideologues walk away from the disaster they have made of public education, the sooner true reform will take place. Parents do not want "equality" in their schools. They want excellence. They want discipline. They want children pressed to the maximum of their abilities, not placed in classrooms where the pace of study is set by the learning level of the slowest student. They want civility, manners, patriotism and morality integrated into the curriculum. And they could not really give a damn less about matters that are of such concern to HEW and the federal judiciary, such as whether the proper black-white teacher ratio has been achieved.

Several years before his untimely death in 1974, the constitutional scholar, Alexander Bickel, provoked a minor uproar with an article in *The New Republic*, the gravamen of which was this: "The actual integration of schools on a significant scale is an enormously difficult undertaking, if a possible one at all. Certainly it creates as many problems as it purports to solve, and no one can be sure that even if accomplished, it would yield an educational return."[4]

The question Professor Bickel was addressing to the educational establishment was basically: Is integration worth the price? In Emily Dickinson's line, is the transport worth the pain?

The burden of proof has shifted to those who believe it is.

IV

Ten years ago, the monumental Coleman Report was published which concluded that the quality of education and the pace of learning depend less on what students find at school,

than on what they bring there. Heredity and home environment were more important to education than the size of the
classroom, the pupil-teacher ratio, the salaries of faculty, or
the physical plant where the child was taught.

Five years ago, the U.S. Office of Education of HEW in a
nationwide survey failed to turn up a single integrated public
school that was free of racial conflict.

Two years ago, in a study of five bussing programs, Harvard sociologist, David Armor, discovered that A) Achievement tests of black students in integrated schools showed no
"significant gains" compared with the achievement levels of
black students in the inner city. B) Grades of black students
fell after transfer to white schools; and so did black aspirations. The aspirations of black children in inner-city schools
were found to be higher than those of blacks in integrated
schools. C) Integration was heightening the "racial identity
and consciousness" of both black and white students; it
tended to "enhance ideologies that promote racial segregation."

Though the conclusions of Armor and other scholars have
startled and angered some educators, they are not really
astonishing to the common man. That bright, upper middle
class parents, black or white, have brighter children than
poor, educationally retarded ones, seems hardly a startling
discovery. Nor is it surprising to learn that inner-city black
children have higher aspirations and do better in school
among other black children than among whites. In many of
the great cities of the nation, Jews, Irish, Italians, Poles,
Puerto Ricans and Indians appear more comfortable and at
ease, living and socializing with their own. Why should not
blacks?

But if the old sociology of the post-war era was reflected in
the decision of 1954, why has not the new sociology been
reflected in the court decisions of the seventies? If compulsory integration, through forced bussing, increases racial animosity and tension, without adding appreciably to the learning
achievement of blacks, how does one justify tearing apart
community after community to achieve it?

For generations now there has beaten within the liberal breast the utopian dream that by placing inner-city black children in schools with white children, the former will quickly pick up the habits and ambitions of the latter—even as they might the Hong Kong flu. Racial amity will be advanced, and racial peace assured.

It does not work—too often, the opposite is occurring.

In the City of Boston, U.S. District Judge W. Arthur Garrity, Jr.'s bussing order, upheld by the Supreme Court, has produced, in the judgment of one *Wall Street Journal* reporter who studied its consequences, "violence that has . . . divided blacks and whites in this city as never before."[5] In Inglewood, California, a Supreme Court Judge finally withdrew his bussing order after more than two-thirds of the white student population fled, following its imposition in 1970. Forced integration, like prohibition, is "an experiment noble in purpose" that has failed. The promised dividends are nowhere in sight. Yet, look at the cost.

Schools like Dunbar are sacrificed on the altar of this Moloch of egalitarianism. Whites by the hundreds of thousands flee the cities and the city schools. Middle-class blacks follow, making of the public schools literal dumping grounds where the only children who remain are those who cannot afford to get out. Bitterness between the races increases. Division in the nation deepens. And white parents go into the streets to fight court orders shipping their children off to distant, alien communities.

Unless the liberals have in mind delivering up the country to Governor Wallace in 1976, the madness seems without method.

In the Brown decision, the late Chief Justice declared, "In approaching this problem, we cannot turn the clock back to 1868 when the Amendment was adopted, or even to 1896 when *Plessy v. Ferguson* was written. We must consider public education in the light of its full development, and its present place in American life throughout the nation."

In 1975, we cannot turn the clock back to 1954. We must today consider public education in the "light of its full development, and its present place in American life . . ." To ignore the lessons of ten years, to plunge ahead with bussing and forced integration, is to fulfill Santayana's definition of the fanatic as the man who redoubles his effort when he has lost sight of his goal.

To the zealots now pressing the courts for cross-county, as well as cross-city, bussing, one implores, in the words of Cromwell in a letter to the Church of Scotland, "My brethren, I beseech you, in the bowels of Christ, think it possible you may be mistaken."

V

A common conclusion of the Coleman Report, and studies by other scholars such as Harvard's Christopher Jencks and the Rand Corporation's Harvey Averch is that the level of spending on public education has next to nothing to do with pupil achievement. Which raises a very hard question. Just what have the taxpayers been getting in return for the added tens of billions of dollars they have poured into education this past decade?

The figures are astounding. In his new book, *The Real America*, Mr. Ben Wattenberg, who can lyricize for a full page on the liberating aspects of the McDonald's Hamburger Stand, cheerfully reports the following:

Spending for education in the U.S. rose from $9 billion in 1950 to $25 billion in 1960 to $86 billion in 1972. Per pupil expenditures went from $378 in 1950 to $546 in 1960 to $828 in 1969 to $1,026 in 1972. According to William F. Buckley's calculations, where thirty years ago education consumed only 2 percent of the Gross National Product, today it consumes 8 percent, more than national defense.

Where did all that money go; where is it going?

Certainly, in the sixties, billions went for the construction of schools, buildings, classrooms and modern facilities to educate the children of the postwar baby boom in the kind of comfort and conditions their parents never knew. Additional billions went to train teachers and reduce the size of the average classroom. Still other funds went toward raising the income of teachers to a level more commensurate with their contribution to society, and to the nation's future. Some two out of every three dollars poured into "education" today, it is said, goes for teachers' salaries.

But, the question arises: If, as Coleman and the others contend, there is no correlation between teachers' salaries and student achievement levels, what are the arguments for more billions for education?

And what does America have to show for the incredible investment of a decade, other than bricks and mortar?

As columnist Jenkin Lloyd Jones writes, "Between 1963 and 1974 the average score on College Entrance Examination Board aptitude tests in the use of English has gone from 478 to 443. The composition score on American College Testing Program has slipped from 19.9 to 18.8."[6]

The more that American taxpayers spend on public education, it appears, the less well educated are the children emerging from the public schools.

Again, Washington, D.C. is a case in point. Twenty-five years ago, the city was investing $256 per pupil per year and the public schools ran the gamut from average to excellent. By 1960 this figure had risen to $431. By 1975, the figure had gone to near $1,600, an increase of almost 400 percent in 15 years. Yet, what were Washingtonians getting for this generous contribution to the education of children? Here is the assessment by an urban analyst writing for *Fortune* Magazine:

> The public school system is a shambles. Violence is commonplace. Absenteeism in the upper grades averages 21 percent. The cost of replacing broken windows comes to $620,000 a year. Even so, it is not uncommon to see school windows boarded up for months until repair crews get around to fixing them.
>
> Pupil achievement on standard tests has been consistently low. Tests in recent years indicate that the achievement level of the average high-school student in

Washington is two grades or more below the national average in reading and vocabulary.

Administrative incompetence has aggravated the problems of the schools. Deliveries on books and other supplies are often weeks late in reaching the classrooms. Teachers' paychecks are issued late and are frequently drawn in incorrect amounts. Father Raymond Kemp, a Roman Catholic priest and a member of the school board says bluntly, 'The demoralized teaching staff has given up in many cases. Their level of expectations has declined to the point where they only hope to get through the year without being mugged, raped or forced to commit sodomy.'[7]

This is the story of public education in the nation's capital with one of the highest per capita pupil expenditures in the United States. Nor is it an uncommon story. According to the Senate Subcommittee on Juvenile Delinquency, by 1973, 70,000 serious assaults were being reported annually against public school teachers; and school disorders had "reached a crisis level that threatened the schools educational mission."

Where is Mr. Nader when we really need him? If a cereal company skimped on the corn flakes in a king-size box, the matter would merit national attention. Where are the consumer champions to alert the nation that the tens of billions being poured into our public schools is not buying superior education. Indeed, in some cases the quality of education is infinitely worse than they themselves received in the little red schoolhouses of their childhood.

If there is a taxpayer's revolt going on in this country, defeating bond issue after bond issue, the surprise is that it has taken so long to get underway.

Consider the figures. Since 1968, the number of public school children between kindergarten and eighth grade has held steady, at just about 32 million. With the declining birth rate, this figure will begin to drop. Some of the more than 3.5 million teachers in the nation's inventory will simply not be needed in public education.

The only remaining argument for increasing education budgets at state, local and federal level is to improve the life style of teachers. And, considering the economic advances teachers—with the rest of the public sector—have made in the last decade, as long as the private sector is suffering, that argument is not good enough.

"Education" is one of those old respected trade marks, belonging to a firm that built up decades of good will, that has been captured and exploited by hustlers.

An October, 1974 essay, in *The Wall Street Journal*, entitled, "Mr. Chips At the Polling Booth," is instructive.

> After years of activity in lobbying, the nation's major teachers' organizations now are moving into "political action"—supporting, staffing and helping to finance electoral campaigns. Worried about threats to school financing and the loss of teaching jobs, the teachers are throwing unprecedented amounts of money and manpower into next month's local, state and national elections.
>
> . . . Their ultimate aim is to win huge increases in federal aid to education, and thus help protect teaching jobs.[8]

As Walter Mossberg, author of the piece, writes, the objective of the National Educational Association is to increase the federal share of the nation's education budget from 7 percent to 33 percent—a transfer of $20 billion from taxpayers to educators.

What the lobbyists of the NEA have in mind is an end run around democracy. Local taxpayers, having caught on to the game, are resisting further tax increases for education. So the NEA is determined to use its political muscle with the Ninety-fourth Congress it helped elect to extract from the U.S. Treasury the billions it cannot raise in its home communities. What is underway here is what the children call a "rip-off."

It will not succeed without the collaboration, or at least

the acquiescence, of the press. Only the national press has the kilowatts to expose NEA's fraudulent claim that the additional funds are "essential for the education of our children," and to publicize the links between those congressmen benefiting from NEA campaign assistance, and those congressmen carrying the hod.

There are educational reforms that might well make of our public schools what they once were, places parents were anxious to have their children enter, not places from which, desperately, they seek escape. These reforms would not cost a dime. They involve restoring practices that prevailed and worked decades ago. They involve setting standards of performance for teachers and students alike, and dismissing those who do not measure up. The schools cannot serve as both educational institutions and reform schools for delinquents. They involve getting back to basics like grammar and math, forgetting for a while about George Jackson, "relevance" and advanced sex education. Taxpayers would do well to adopt a policy of not one more penny for education until such reforms are made.

VI

The integrationist impulse which captivates the minority which has captured much of the bureaucratic and judicial power in America is not restricted to education. When open housing legislation failed to produce the desired measure of integration in the suburbs, government decided to bring it about, by fiat. Behind the policy of "scatter-site" housing lies the conviction that a new address means a new man. Slum dwellers, scooped up out of Bedford Stuyvesant, say, and set down alongside middle-class whites will quickly get the hang of the thing, and become similar in outlook, attitude and lifestyle. Thereby will the problems of inner-city poverty be solved.

Reinhold Niebuhr has referred to this charming notion as "the doctrine of salvation by bricks."

It has not succeeded in its objective; but it has succeeded in adding to the already considerable deposits of racial bitterness in America. The reasons are not distant.

As Professor Edward Banfield has pointed out, to the distress of his academic colleagues, poverty is not simply an economic condition. It is often the consequence of a particular perspective on life, a perspective that is not changed by changing one's zip code. Slum people taken out of slums, put into public housing, have quickly recreated the environment they recently left. Forgotten, too often, is that slums are not built by contractors; they are created by people—people without ambition, people without hope, but, nevertheless, people. As evidence has shown, the wholesale transfer of slum populations into middle-class neighborhoods is less likely to uplift the former than to radicalize the latter.

Consider Forest Hills. Here was a peaceful Jewish community in Queens County which, it was decided by Manhattan's city planners, would provide an ideal setting for the latest adventure in progress of the then Mayor of New York, John Lindsay. Forest Hills was to be rewarded for its liberalism with a spanking new 840-unit public housing project. Having escaped the blessings of proximity to such massive projects in Manhattan, many Jews in Forest Hills became decidedly illiberal, and, in the eyes of some, downright reactionary.

But the Jews were right. Why is it that Government can be so eternally solicitous of the physical environment of a handful of Alaskan caribou, and so ham-fisted in rearranging the social environment people have created in their own communities?

Deciding the racial or ethnic composition of neighborhoods is not the business of government. It should be the consequence of the free choice of individuals. And if those choices result in ethnic, religious or racial enclaves, government should scrupulously respect those decisions. Life in an integrated community is one way of life. Who is to dictate that, in this heterogeneous society, that it is the only way or even the best way?

The Little Italys, the Chinatowns, the Irish, Polish, Jewish and other ethnic communities of the nation's cities are not social problems. They are part of the heritage, part of the strength, of America. The social problem crying out for relief is the existence of a minority of zealots, with disproportionate power, who will not desist from using government to coerce people into involuntary social associations they do not want.

This country has never voted government a franchise to bring about racial, religious, ethnic or class integration. And until the "reformers," bent upon such purposes, are replaced, the country will not know social peace. Regrettably, they have never learned what Malcolm X discovered as a young man:

> I tucked it into my mind that when I returned home I would tell Americans this observation; that where true brotherhood existed among all colors, where no one felt segregated, where there was no "superiority" complex, no "inferiority" complex—then voluntarily, naturally, people of the same kind felt drawn together by that which they had in common.[10]

VII

The most recent of the "second generation" of demands is, of course, for "quotas." Equal access to jobs and promotion and hiring lists is to be replaced by a fixed percentage, regardless of qualification or experience.

The theory is that, had it not been for two centuries of slavery and one century of second-class citizenship, blacks would have advanced to the point where they could have won these jobs on their own—ergo, justice dictates that they be provided with them now.

In practice, however, this requires a policy of reverse discrimination against white males every bit as invidious and odious as that which preceded it.

For decades blacks were denied the right to vote, denied the right to participate in professional sports. But, does anyone today suggest that blacks should have two votes to make up for past discrimination, or that blacks should have a fixed percentage of positions on every professional hockey or football team in the nation? Such would be ludicrous. Yet, if Americans would not tolerate lowering the standards of their professional sports, why should they tolerate, for example, a lowering of the standards of scholarship in their colleges and universities?

When one includes women, blacks, Spanish-speaking Americans and others, at least 60 percent of the country is now designated "minority" for purposes of preferential hiring. Some minorities, however, like Jews, Catholics, Irish, and Poles have been cut from the preferred list. But many of these groups have themselves been victimized by discrimination. Why should Americans, whose great-grandparents came to this country to escape famine, pogroms, poverty and persecution, now submit to discrimination in favor of Americans whose great-grandparents were slaves?

The immigrants did not bring slavery or segregation to America; they found it when they arrived.

Nor can it really be said that young blacks in this country, the principal beneficiaries of these policies, are all that impoverished or discriminated against.

According to the latest census, outside the South, the income of the average black family where the head of the household was under 35 had reached 93 percent of white income. Where both husband and wife worked, the black family income was 105 percent of the average white. Young non-Southern blacks in America are at, or approaching, the same income level as whites. Where is the justice in discriminating, in their behalf, against ethnic minorities further down the ladder of success?

"Life," President Kennedy said, "is unfair." Certainly, history has been cruel to blacks. But that history cannot be erased by replacing old injustices with new ones.

Like other social policies, this reverse discrimination was never debated and voted outright by Congress. It is a policy imposed by bureaucrats who have twisted the intent and purpose of executive and agency orders, and whom the politicians dare not defy for fear of being labeled "racist." In truth, however, some of the most systematic and widespread practices of racism in America are being done by the Government of the United States.

Businesses that have balked at federal orders to hire more blacks have been threatened with loss of contracts. Colleges and universities that have insisted that the standards of merit, scholarship and achievement must apply have been threatened with a cut-off of federal funds. For many universities, that threat is mortal.

Some academics are beginning to understand what it was conservatives meant when they warned a decade ago that "federal funds mean federal control." Above all the weeping and gnashing of teeth in the groves of academe today, about the tyrannical character of HEW, one hears the unmistakable sound of chickens coming home to roost.

Few teachers in city schools today do not know a colleague who was passed over for principal because he was not of the preferred minority. Few employees in the Washington bureaucracy do not have a tale of how blacks or women were hired or advanced over a score of civil servants, to meet the demands of higher-ups.

Washington is truly the capital of hypocrisy. The air echoes with the cries of "shame," that Mr. Nixon's men may have violated the virginity of the civil service by seeding the bureaucracy with personnel chosen not for ability, but political loyalty. Yet, when blacks or women are moved into government offices, when they are jumped over men with a lifetime of public service, men with greater experience and ability, there is not a whimper of protest about the rape of the merit system, because the crime is committed in a good cause.

Despite the country's drift to the right on social issues, there seems little hope of restraining the government machinery now in operation in the bureaucracy and the courts. Even as HEW draws up, and the courts hand down, bussing orders that turn Democratic precincts overnight into Wallace precincts, Congress is paralyzed. The reasons are several.

As the cave-in at the Kansas City mini-convention demonstrated, the Democratic Party is dominated by liberals psychologically and politically hostage to the blacks, who are in turn responsive to a leadership that equates compromise with moral cowardice. As for the modern Republicans, their eternal fear is that they will be charged with being "insensitive," or worse, "racist." Rather than tear up the pea patch, and crack down upon its own bureaucracy, the Republican White House, like its predecessor, prefers to let them be about their business.

Indeed, after the success the McGovern Convention of '72 had with quotas, the Republican Party was in 1974 busy drafting an "affirmative action" program of its own for future GOP conventions—providing us with supporting evidence, if any were needed, of the validity of John Stuart Mills' observation that the Tories are "the stupid party."

VIII

What needs to be done is nothing less than to ring down the curtain on the Second Reconstruction. The nation needs to return to the letter and spirit of the Brown decision of 1954 and the Civil Rights Act of 1964. State-imposed or state-subsidized discrimination would be outlawed, but integration would not be mandated.

As Bickel wrote, the federal courts of this country have fallen short of the hopes of De Tocqueville that they would learn "how to understand the spirit of the age, how to confront those obstacles that can be overcome, and to steer out of the current when the tide threatens to carry them away . . ."[11]

The nation needs to be rescued from the consequences of the Green decision and its progeny. And the Supreme Court needs to be pulled out of the current, as the tide threatens to carry it away. A constitutional amendment appears the only way out, affirming Brown and overturning Green, denying the Government of the United States or any state the right to use race as a criterion in the assignment of children to the public schools.

Secondly, the bureaucracy could be readily stripped by Congress of the power to withhold funds from primary and secondary schools which refused to keep records of the racial, religious, ethnic or sexual composition of their classrooms. This would remove the federal courts and the federal bureaucracy from the problems of local school districts, which they have done less to resolve than to aggravate, at enormous cost to us all. Third, the federal machinery needs to be dismantled.

It is not enough to execute publicly, every two years, a Leon Panetta or a Stanley Pottinger. Washington and the bureaucracy are crawling with potential martyrs, who would salivate over the chance to win the prestige, publicity, plaudits and guaranteed careers this most liberal of cities provides automatically to those who manage to get themselves fired for zealotry in the cause of "civil rights." And anyone who believes that by changing an Assistant Secretary at HEW one changes policy has not been there.

Under Presidents Johnson and Nixon, the civil rights enforcement machinery at the Equal Employment Opportunity Commission, the office of federal contract compliance at Labor, the civil rights divisions at Justice and HEW, and the Civil Rights Commission itself have all been strengthened and expanded.

Compulsory integration, and reverse discrimination, will remain the policy of government until this vast and complex machine is deprived of the fuel upon which it runs, i.e., the tax dollars of the American people, which it annually consumes by the hundreds of millions.

As for an end to racial conflict in America, the first step along that road is to make the government of the United States color-blind.

☆

Can Democracy Survive the New Journalism?

I

The political power of America's media monopolies such as CBS, Time-Life, Inc. and the Washington Post Company—welded to the growing ideological fervor of their correspondents, writers and commentators—represents the most formidable obstacle in the path of a conservative counter-reformation in the United States.

It was the concentrated firepower of the national press which sustained the civil rights revolution; and it was the nation's big media which consciously destroyed public support for the American cause in Southeast Asia. It was the national press which lifted Hubert Humphrey up by his bootstraps after the Salt Lake City speech in late September of 1968, enabling him to recover from the Chicago disaster; and it was the abandonment of George McGovern by the liberal press which guaranteed that his defeat would be an unprecedented rout.

Without the sustained support of the media monopolies, for its basic positions, the national Democratic Party, which has succeeded only once since 1944 in winning a clear presidential majority, would be an unimpressive adversary. And without the steady stream of favorable publicity they provide for the priorities, programs and politicians of the left, Government in this country would long ago have begun to reflect the rightward drift in the body politic.

Members of the national press corps prefer to be considered servants of truth, rather than wielders of power. But, as the political historian Theodore H. White has observed:

> The power of the press in America is a primordial one. It sets the agenda of public discussion; and this sweeping political power is unrestrained by any law. It determines what people will talk and think about—an authority that in other nations is reserved for tyrants, priests, parties, and mandarins.[1]

The press determines what "people will talk and think about" because of the monopoly it holds over the news and information flowing out of Washington, capital of the West. That monopoly is as serious a matter for democracy as Arab control of the Mideast oil is for the economies of Western Europe. For what oil is to an industrial nation, accurate information is to a democracy—its lifeblood.

The essence of press power lies in the authority to select, elevate and promote one set of ideas, issues and personalities —and to ignore others.

As Douglass Cater wrote a decade and a half ago:

> The power they exercise is continuing and substantive. They are the articulators of those events of government which they and their bosses deem worthy of note. Their strength stems from their ability to select—to define what is news and what isn't. In Washington on an average day, a good many hundreds of thousands of words are spoken, tens of dozens of "events" occur. The press decides which of those words and events shall receive the prompt attention of millions, and which, like timber falling in a deep and uninhabited forest, shall crash silently to the ground.[2]

That this "ability to select—to define what is news and what isn't," is an extraordinary power can be ascertained by considering how the most powerful of the network news organizations, CBS, informed its viewers on matters of war and national security. During 1972 and 1973, in America's final year in Vietnam, CBS had 521 evening news shows covering 196 hours of broadcasting. In that period:

· "Doves" urging more rapid U.S. withdrawal received more than twenty-five times the coverage of those arguing for more vigorous military action.

· The only belligerent to receive favorable coverage, on balance, was Hanoi. CBS' treatment of the U.S.-South Vietnamese war effort was negative by a margin of four-to-one.

· Soviet advances in strategic weapons received just five minutes of attention in 196 hours of programming.

· The shifting balance of power against the U.S., toward the Soviets, got one minute of attention in two years.

· Two-thirds of all coverage of the U.S. armed forces was negative. The heroism of U.S. soldiers in Vietnam was largely ignored. Emphasis was focused on the fragging of officers, atrocity stories, alleged racism and sexism in the ranks, cost over-runs, and unauthorized bombings.

· Americans favoring "detente" with Moscow and Peking received between fifteen and twenty-five times the footage of Americans skeptical or opposed to U.S. policy.

These conclusions emerged from a sentence-by-sentence analysis of two years of transcripts of CBS Evening News by foreign policy scholar Dr. Ernest W. Lefever of the Brookings Institution.[3] When released, his report was ignored by the networks, was granted ten paragraphs on page six of the B Section of *The Washington Post*, and relegated to page 75 in the *New York Times*. Though the *Post*, and other publications, have done back-page analyses, not one in a thousand Americans is probably aware of the Lefever Report, its contents and implications.

Some two-thirds of the nation depends upon the networks as the primary source of information about government, issues and politics. If one set of facts, one side of the question of war, peace and security is rarely heard, how are the American people to make wise judgments upon matters that may affect the life and death of nations, not excluding their own?

II

The political bias of the Washington press, which affects both the selection of stories and the character of coverage, is a matter about which distinguished members of the national press, like Howard K. Smith and Robert Novak, have themselves written. Below are but a few trademarks of the New Journalism:

First, poet-Vietnam, there is a discernible anti-military bias permeating what is spoken and written by the national press. Politicians and diplomats play upon this bias as upon a violin. When the second Moscow summit failed to produce dramatic progress on strategic arms, the Secretary of State knew he would have a receptive audience in the press for his suggestion that the military establishments of both sides were the stumbling block. For the press corps is a community which by-and-large views the United States strategic weapons inventory as less reflective of the security needs of the nation than of the political leverage of the "military-industrial complex."

The anti-military sentiment aids in understanding why a President cannot propose a dime's worth of cuts in social programs without a chorus of press inquiries as to how much is being cut from defense. Braced with the Lefever Report, documenting the rank bias of his CBS Evening News against conservative views on national security, Mr. Walter Cronkite airily dismissed his questioner: "There are always groups in Washington expressing views of alarm over the state of our defense. *We don't carry those stories.* The story is that there are those who want to cut defense spending."[4] Few more pristine examples of the mentality of the New Journalism may be found. And it is because they play to the anti-Pentagon bias in the national press that young congressmen like Les Aspin are afforded such sympathetic coverage.

Second, the new journalist bears a Naderite grudge against big business. To him, tax reform means hiking the corporate levy and socking it to the oil companies. The rare appearances which businessmen make upon the network news almost invariably have to do with their being charged with fouling the air or polluting the water, profiteering at the public expense, or corrupting the political process. What makes this selective treatment of U.S. business ironic is that the metropolitan press and the networks depend upon corporate advertising to survive. With its steady encouragement of government regulation of business, the media is siding with the single political power that can one day threaten its own income, independence and freedom.

Third, the media has a bias for federal social spending; the more, the better. In Mr. Nixon's White House, it was predictable as the rising sun that a proposed cut in social spending would generate a network report on how brilliantly the affected program had been working, and what untold suffering would assuredly ensue were it cut. Whether legal services, hospital construction or federal day-care centers, the networks found it obligatory to produce sympathetic footage designed to make the proponent of spending reductions appear a lineal descendent of Simon Legree.

A textbook example of the technique was available on the tenth of January 1975 when CBS mounted a counter-attack against President Ford's proposal to reduce the federal cost of food stamps.

Where around three million were being fed on food stamps when Mr. Nixon took office, by the first month of 1975 that figure had risen to more than 17 million—and the cost was up some 2,000 percent to almost $4 billion. Unless something was done, it was predicted that some 50 to 60 million could be participating by 1977 at a cost to the taxpayers of $10 billion annually. This, of course, was not exactly what Presidents Kennedy and Johnson had in mind when they initiated the pilot food stamp program in the sixties to help the neediest of Americans meet their nutritional needs.

According to the CBS report—from Little Rock by correspondent Ed Rabel—Mr. Ford's scheme appeared designed to shove the poor of America directly into starvation. No presentation was made of the President's persuasive case. Rather, we were treated to a dramatized, indeed sensationalized, account of the untold suffering to follow if three families had to pay 30 percent, rather than 23 percent of net income for subsidized food.

"The Administration says its plan would save the country $645 million, but the critics believe the savings would risk massive malnutrition and possible starvation." Neither Rabel nor his "sources" explained why these people had not starved to death before the food stamp program exploded under President Nixon.

In any event, as the President's case was never effectively presented by the national news media, the President lost in Congress by a landslide. And so it goes.

There is a reverse side to this boundless enthusiasm for federal social action. It is the national press' indifference to what is done on the state and local level, especially by privately supported institutions, and voluntary associations, such as the Boys' Club or the Red Cross. The big media has no interest in the alternatives to the welfare state.

Fourth, there is an abiding conviction that no matter the controversy or conflict involved, the federal government should continue to use its coercive powers to integrate schools and communities. Like civil rights leaders, the press views this as a moral issue. Trimming here is not politics as usual. It is "courting racist votes," and "appealing to the worst instincts of the American people." Opponents of quotas or bussing are ever walking on eggshells in trepidation of being so labeled. Meanwhile, the integrationist, no matter how silly or extreme his proposition, is at worst adjudged a misguided idealist ahead of his time.

Fifth, the national press is the silent partner of the political and social movements of liberalism—consumerism, civil rights, environmental, anti-war and womens' liberation. The successes of these enterprises are regarded as "victories" for social justice, progress and the quality of life. Defeats are invariably "setbacks" on the road to inevitable triumph. For the zealots and extremists of these fashionable movements, the national press shows an extraordinary measure of tolerance.

Had it been Birchers, instead of the Black Panthers, who announced a breakfast-for-orphans program or local ambulance service, there would have been none of the return-of-the-Prodigal-Son publicity lavished on the latter. Had it been Youth for Wallace rather than anti-war children who trashed Georgetown on May Day, there would have been no media outrage over police failure to fill out properly the arrest forms. Had it been the KKK, instead of the feathered hoodlums of the AIM, who seized and pillaged the Bureau of Indian Affairs, there would have been no calls for "understanding," no toleration of the $66,000 White House bribe to get the thugs out of town. Often, it is tea and sympathy for the crazies of the left; while for the rednecks who get obstreperous, federal marshals and federal troops.

III

Structure is policy, Richard Goodwin once noted and there is validity in the observation. Beyond any political prejudice of Washington reporters, there are also structural and institutional biases built into the networks, which affect "the news" that emerges.

The first is location. The principal bureaus from which emanate probably four of every five stories on the evening news are located in Los Angeles, Chicago, New York and Washington. Heavily Democratic, these communities are caught up with the politics of the city, the politics of race, the politics of protest. Most of the network news originates from New York and Washington, towns dominated by the most powerful liberal press in the nation—upon which publications, anchormen, commentators and correspondents alike depend for ideas, leads and intellectual sustenance.

Were the networks to originate programming from, say, Birmingham, Alabama, the "national news" might reflect more the priorities of the Birmingham press and the concerns of the people of Alabama, rather than the priorities of the *Washington Post* and the concerns of midtown Manhattan.

The location of major network news bureaus helps one to understand another phenomenom of American politics, the rise of senators, and even congressmen, as potential presidential candidates, and the decline of the governors. To air the views, nationally, of a Kennedy, a Percy, a Jackson or a Mo Udall requires of a network crew the investment of only a few minutes time to make the film on the Hill and a short ride downtown to the studio to process it. To air, nationally, the views of Reuben Askew, or Dolph Briscoe or Meldrin Thompson, governors of their respective states, might require of a network thousands of dollars in either air travel or cable costs. Accessibility is all important. Because they are in business to make money, the networks do not invest time or funds necessary to provide the country, regularly, with the views of the governors on breaking national issues. Senators and congressmen, however, congregated in Washington, have easy access to the airwaves. Thus, it is that Congressman John Brademas, who represents 9 percent of the State of Indiana, is better known to the American people than any of the last nine governors of the Hoosier State.

A second factor affecting the shape of television news is that of time. In the *Times* or *Post*, a significant and complex story might run on for columns. A network news report, however, must be forced into a time frame of seconds, or at most a few minutes. A full transcript of the "evening news" would not take up even a single page in the *New York Times*.

When the ads are considered, each evening news show has only twenty-two or twenty-three minutes of news broadcasting. A large fraction of that is consumed by the anchorman; the balance is divided among the bureaus where it is subdivided among competing correspondents. Within the Washington bureau which may have six or seven minutes of air time, competition for an additional forty-five seconds can be fierce. What does this do to the shape of the stories carried?

Necessarily, these abbreviated reports must be shallow. Nuance, shading, explanation must be ruthlessly shucked off, and what remains is often bare bones, simplistic and incomplete. All the arguments made against the sixty-second and the two-minute spot political commercial can be made with equal cogency against many network news reports.

Consider the minimum wage. For many years, conservative economists have argued that the correlation between a high minimum wage and high unemployment among the unskilled is absolute. Others contend that increasing the minimum wage not only prices the least able out of the job market, but threatens others, because of the incentive it provides to automation. Still others view rapid advances in the minimum wage as socially devastating in the inner city, especially to black teenagers who need work experience infinitely more than they need the higher wage few employers will pay a seventeen-year-old.

In brief, the minimum wage is anything but a simple issue. Yet, what comes across the networks is that, "Senator Kennedy and the Democrats called today for a 20-cent increase in the minimum wage; the Republican Administration, however, is opposed, arguing that raising the income of the poorest-paid workers will mean added unemployment.

The narrowed time frame, which forces controversial issues into the for-against format is tailor-made for the political liberal. He identifies a "problem," has a "program," to provide a "solution." The conservative, meanwhile, is inevitably cast in the role of negativist, or oppositionist.

Still, another occupational bias is that, by definition, newsmen are interested in "news." They seek out what is changing not what endures. What St. Paul said of the Athenians is descriptive of journalists, "For all the Athenians and strangers which were there spent their time in nothing else, but either to tell or to hear some new thing."[5]

In Mr. Nixon's years the White House press corps would campaign in print and on the air for a presidential press conference. When the conference came and went, they would pronounce themselves satisfied or disappointed, depending on whether there was "news" in it. How well their occupational appetite for something new to say or write was satiated was the yardstick they used to judge the utility of the conference.

The same yardstick was applied to foreign policy addresses. Perhaps the most important speech of the Nixon years was the November 3, 1969, "great silent majority" address—at the height of the anti-war fever and demonstrations—to rally the nation behind his Vietnam policy. Prior to air time, Dr. Kissinger went to the Hill to brief the Republican leadership. The following colloquy recounted by William Safire in *Before the Fall* is here instructive:

> After Kissinger finished his resume of the speech, Senator Hugh Scott asked, "The TV people will ask me, 'What's new in it?' What's the answer."[6]
> Henry shot back: "The answer is not what's new but what's right."

But the answer was unsatisfactory to a national press which continued to criticize President Nixon's Vietnam speeches—even as they had President Johnson's—because there was "nothing new" in them, "no new approaches to Hanoi," "no new concessions" at Paris. To some reporters it seemed to make little difference whether the American peace offer on the table was just or magnanimous—or whether the best policy was to stand our ground. Their professional need for "news" could not be satisfied without regular changes in the American position.

When this craving to "hear or tell some new thing" is harnessed to a medium with the insatiable appetite of the network news, tremendous pressures are created upon politicians, diplomats, executives and negotiators for movement and change where none may be warranted. And because liberals are never without a "bold new program"—and the conservative may believe that when it is not necessary to change, it is necessary not to change—the former is customarily better copy than the latter.

A final institutional bias toward the left arises from the competitive character of television journalism. The princely salaries of the television newsmen depend upon the huge advertising revenues which in turn depend upon Nielsen ratings. These ratings require the winning and holding of an audience of millions of viewers, whose educational level is perhaps eleventh grade, whose fickleness is legendary, whose boredom threshold is remarkably low.

Either the network news is captivating and entertaining or its ratings begin to fall, in which event the executives and editors—no matter the quality of the show—begin casting about for a new "team."

The entertainment imperative, the need always to be exciting and controversial, rather than any political bias, some scholars argue, explains televisions's preference for militants, demonstrators, extremists and freaks. It is an entertainment not a news medium, they argue. Therefore, it must always prefer the bizarre antics of a Bella Abzug to the legislative achievements of an Edith Green.

And it is this craving for controversy that explains why the camera must prefer the heretic to the established church, the dissenter to the conformist, the assailant of institutions to the officials of those institutions.

As the addict needs his fix, as the prime time show needs its dosage of sex and violence, so the network news must have its drama, its controversy, its excitement. Were there no conflicts in American society to report, the network news would have to invent them.

IV

Two other aspects of the new journalism should not go unmentioned. First is the Washington correspondent's insistence that his is an "adversary relationship" with the men in power; second, the chronic negativism that pervades coverage of American society.

Between Presidents and the press there has always been an adversary relationship. Before the modern era, however, it was a tension arising out of the press' desire for "news," and government's penchant for confidentiality and secrecy. Today's adversary relationship is more nearly the genuine article.

The Washington press corps today views itself less as the "Fourth Branch of Government" than as a separate center of moral and political authority independent of and in opposition to the party in power.

Especially in the aftermath of Watergate, the new journalist has come to see himself as not simply a recorder, but a shaper of events, the chosen surrogate of the American people in the corridors of power, the guardian of the Republic. Believing himself the moral, intellectual and political equal or superior of the politicians he covers, he is less reticent than ever about passing judgment.

Yet, in this adversary relationship in which the new journalist takes such pride there is as much fraud as truth. The Washington press was the adversary of Presidents Nixon and Johnson on the war in Vietnam. They were not adversaries when it came to Mr. Johnson's Great Society or Mr. Nixon's Family Assistance Plan. And while the Washington press considers itself in an adversary relationship with The White House, it is less adversary than acolyte of the 75 freshmen Democrats in the House. The adversary relationship is a stance the modern journalist adopts not toward the whole government but toward selected officials and agencies.

With congressional staffers and legislators anxious to block Administration spending cuts, with bureaucrats disloyal to the President, the new journalist is no adversary. He is often friend, collaborator, and, if you will, co-conspirator. Formerly, the press cultivated official sources who could predict, explain and defend U.S. policy. The new journalist prefers sources who will oppose or frustrate policy, who will help expose and embarrass government. The old arrangements—

confidentiality in exchange for a story, with the reporter getting the byline and the bureaucrat airing his views anonymously—remain.

That adversary journalism is in vogue is evident in the Pulitzer Prizes. In the forties, it was war correspondents like Ernie Pyle and cartoonists like Bill Mauldin, who celebrated the humanity and heroism of the G.I., who won the awards. During Vietnam, the Pulitzers went to journalists who uncovered hidden American atrocities or newspapers which published classified documents, leaked to discredit and damage the war effort.

What makes adversary journalism a serious problem for democracy is that the press controls the channel of communication between government and governed. If that channel is cluttered with the opinions, biases, and prejudices of adversary journalists, how is government to communicate with the people? A government that cannot communicate cannot lead. And government that cannot lead cannot survive.

In assuming this adversary role, reporters and correspondents are neglecting the indispensable duty they perform in a democratic society; i.e., to serve as the reliable transmission belt between the elected and chosen leaders of the nation, and the nation itself. Reporters may not like and may not agree with the arguments of government or the statements of political leaders, but if they do not record them accurately and report them faithfully, who else will do the job? And, again, if political leaders and government leaders cannot communicate, regularly and directly with the citizens, how can democracy endure?

Reporters are increasingly reluctant to play this central role that is theirs. We are not simply stenographers, they argue. We are not parrots. We are not the echo chamber of the politicians. We will no longer relay faithfully the lies of politicians, or the propaganda of government. We will decide whether the messages sent by the men in power in Washington are even worth delivering. In this attitude, there is genuine trouble brewing for the Republic.

If journalists decide that they alone will determine in what context government decisions and statements are reported to the nation, they should expect increasing demands from presidents for direct access to the people, over the airwaves. And the newsman who defines his role as an adversary of government should not be surprised when the White House reciprocates, and assumes its own adversary stance toward the national press.

Lastly, though it claims to "hold up a mirror" to society, the press, and in particular the networks, is in reality a powerful searchlight, which focuses, disproportionately, upon what is wrong with America. Eric Sevareid argues that this must necessarily be so, since the one plane that crashes is more newsworthy than the thousand that land safely.

But the chronic negativism that is almost a defining characteristic of the new journalism cannot be brushed aside with Mr. Cronkite's regal wave of the hand, "I don't think it is any of our business what the moral, political, social or economic effect of our reporting is."

For clearly, the American people are beginning to feel its debilitating effects. According to William Watts and Lloyd Free, authors of *State of the Nation*, Americans are sanguine about their personal futures but increasingly apprehensive about the future of their society and system. This is the country they see, not first-hand, but nightly through their television screens. It is a nation more malnourished and hungry than the one in which they live. It is a land where labor and management are regularly at sword's point, where race relations are rarely tranquil, where the public schools are always embroiled in controversies over bussing or textbooks, where the armed forces are awash in drugs, sexism and racism. The America of the network news is not the nation two hundred million Americans reside in.

Yet, when Mr. Cronkite closes his half-hour, he does not tell us that we have witnessed a few bizarre and atypical episodes of the day in an otherwise tranquil and prosperous Republic. Rather he intones, "and that's the way it is."

Once, it was a hallmark of Americans that they were brash, cocky and confident. Readily, they declared theirs the greatest nation in the history of man. While grating to foreign visitors, surely that spirit helped the United States pull itself out of the great depression while maintaining our free institutions, to crush tyrannies on both sides of the globe, to rebuild the shattered economies of Europe and Japan, and to block Communist aggression, all the while increasing the prosperity of our people.

And, if the sons and daughters of our war generation, living in a more affluent country, cannot equal the sacrifices and achievements of those years, does not partial responsibility lie with the men controlling the media who have endlessly proclaimed to Americans what an unjust, corrupt and rotten society they have produced?

A nation has need of muckrakers. But, as Teddy Roosevelt emphasized, "but only if they know when to stop raking the muck." The marriage of the men of words—with their chronic dissatisfaction with things as they are—to this mighty instrument of mass media may well be the combination which finally breaks the spirit of the American people.

V

The national press seeks the prerogative of the courtesan: power without responsibility. It is not a closed question whether democracy can co-exist with that power.

Consider. Americans believe in dissent; the right is enshrined in the Constitution; legal and peaceful channels have been provided for its expression. Yet, what kind of dissent is it that the networks favor with maximum coverage? Is it the reasoned dissent of the scholar, or the raucous, militant dissent of the political extremist? Do not the networks confer the incomparable rewards of prime time publicity upon those dissenters who make their case with mass demonstrations and disorders? No elected tribal chief in the country has garnered one tenth the publicity that Russell Means and his splinter movement have gotten for pillaging the Bureau of Indian Affairs, and seizing Wounded Knee. Indeed, was their success not the example set for the Menominee Warriors who seized, occupied, and finally, extorted that monastery away from its rightful owners in Wisconsin?

To the networks the more militant the demonstration, the more extreme the protest, the more belligerent the form of dissent, the greater the likelihood it will be aired on the evening news. This structure of rewards is like a giant magnet drawing dissenters away from peaceful and legitimate methods toward the dramatic, the illegal and the undemocratic. Every irresponsible political leader in the country now knows, and knows well, that the road to the front pages, the avenue to the airwaves, is to take your dissent out of the courts and into the streets.

What was it Whitney Young said before he died—Stokely Carmichael's constituency consisted of 50 blacks and 5,000 reporters. It is no coincidence that the era of militant and mass demonstrations corresponds precisely with the growth of electronic journalism.

Most Americans would concur that among the nation's critical needs is the reestablishment of public confidence in our institutions. But how can that confidence be rebuilt when the networks—because they must excite and entertain—must prefer the heretic and the dissident priest to the established Church, the maverick to the party loyalist, the assailants of institutions to the institutions themselves? "It is not the critic who counts," said T. R. in his "Man in the Arena" oration. But to the networks, it *is* the critic who counts. Cynics and wits who will savage individuals, institutions and society in general are infinitely more attractive to the news and talk shows than those who defend and sustain our institutions.

So it is that the venomous assaults on American politics and life, of a Gore Vidal, will always be welcome on the talk shows that would be bored to tears with traditional defenders of the American way of life.

Almost without exception in the last decade, the Presidency, the Courts, the Congress, the FBI, the Department of Justice, the CIA, the business community, the military have declined in the esteem of the American people. Is it not because they have, all of them, been made the subject of regular assault in the news columns and over the airwaves of the nation?

Every institution needs criticism; it is indispensable for renewal. But few institutions can survive constant assault. And when those attacks are harnessed to an engine with the power of network television, there should be no surprise that our institutions are reeling under the blows.

While it may not be the purpose of the networks to tear down confidence in the institutions upon which democracy depends, that is the inevitable result when the networks elevate, promote and publicize the people who attack those institutions. And this the networks do for the single reason that such people, like the freaks at the carnival, attract crowds; and it is upon crowds that the networks depend for their profits.

What of national unity? Surely, network correspondents would concur this is a worthwhile objective to pursue. But how can any president, how could Dwight Eisenhower, have brought Americans together if two-thirds of the nation in the fifties had looked for information about their society to a medium of communication which depended for success and survival upon the volume of conflict, confrontation and controversy it brought to the screen? Week after week, the average American, in front of his television set, is, in effect, asked to take sides, between anti-war demonstrators and hard hats, religious fundamentalists and educational reformers, pro-bussing blacks and anti-bussing Irish, striking miners and coal company officials, liberals and conservatives. Night after night after night, the networks compete with one another in reproducing, for a potential audience of 50 million, the most exciting moment of the most divisive conflict of the day.

America is a divided nation in 1975. And it will remain divided so long as a majority of Americans depend upon network television for news of their society. The "entertainment imperative" of the network news—the need always to be more controversial and conflict-oriented than the competitors—

places the networks in the vanguard of the centrifugal forces pulling America apart.

In the sixties this country entered a new era; and it is not certain how we shall emerge. Democracy needs leaders long on integrity, wisdom, experience and intelligence. The dominant media seeks out "new faces" who are glib, photogenic, charismatic and controversial. Democracy must have its dissent expressed in legal peaceful channels. The networks provide maximum publicity to those who take their grievances outside the law. Democracy needs restored public confidence in its institutions. The networks, to prosper, must favor the cynics and wits who savage and assault those institutions. Democracy, to endure, needs a broad measure of unity among its people. But the networks, to survive, must push before the country, nightly, the most divisive social conflict of the day. Democracy, to survive, needs a broad vital center of politics. But the networks, because they must be controversial, are constantly pulled away from the dull politics of the middle to the exciting politics of the extremes. Democracy needs concurrence, moderation and social peace; the network news thrives on excitement, radical politics and social conflict.

VI

That the conservative and the new journalist should be as mongoose and cobra is not surprising. For the latter's "adversary relationship" is most in evidence when conservative policies are being promoted. And the virtues traditionally prized by conservatives—party fidelity, commitment to principle, respect for traditional values and established institutions, political consistency—are poison to the television news. They need a daily plateful of dissent, action, excitement and drama, which it is fair to say are not customarily the conservative's long suits.

There is a genuine question whether any conservative politician can rivet the camera's attention without ceasing to be, strictly speaking, a conservative. It is worth noting that the one man on the right to capture the greatest network notice in the last decade was Spiro T. Agnew. And he attracted media by assaulting the institutions dominated by the left: the networks, the national press, the academic elite, the Eastern Establishment.

The lesson seems clear. If television responds most immediately and most regularly to the politics of the attack, men of the right should spend less of their time defending their own institutions, and more of their time on the political offensive.

Because of its built-in political bias, the national press will generally ignore conservatives and be taken up with the causes of the fashionable left. But, paradoxically, because of its institutional bias—its constant need to bring raw social conflict into the living rooms of America—the networks will contribute to the national drift to the right.

Again, paradoxically, network correspondents and cameramen have been unwittingly among the foremost recruiters of the American right. All the footage from Harlem, Watts, Newark and Detroit they carried, plus the film of the thuggish anti-war demonstrators of the campus and the Chicago Convention, helped George Wallace roll up 10 million votes in 1968. And the nightly assault upon the sensibilities of middle America by the militant Indians, militant females, militant blacks and militants of all stripes—of whom the networks seem so enamoured—will continue to polarize the nation between left and right.

To suggest that our country would be a more peaceful and unified nation if the networks folded their tents and quietly stole away is to sin against the First Amendment. But it is the truth. The most biased of America's metropolitan newspapers is a less divisive and more comprehensive and informative instrument of communication.

The likelihood of change within the media is not great.

Watergate has convinced the liberal press it was right all along, that the criticism of the Nixon years concerning media prejudice and abuse of power was the diversionary tactic of an Administration which feared the truth. Convinced they rescued the nation from the most monstrous of tyrannies, the dominant press does not even bother to answer its critics now. The old arrogance, put aside in the attic for a few years, has been brought out and dusted off. History, as they say, is written by the winners.

As the veteran reporters retire in the nation's capital, they are replaced by younger men, to whom the new journalism, with its aggressiveness, hostility to officialdom, particular prejudices and point of view, holds open the avenue to the Pulitzer Prizes and Polk awards. And adversary journalism is where the action is. Even the wire services, the last bastions of traditional reporting, are no longer immune.

Many journalists in this capital are as concerned as media critics over what all this portends for the future of their country and their craft. But they are in the minority, and less and less outspoken in their concerns. And even though most of the nation's newspapers, off the Boston-New York-Washington axis, remain moderate or conservative in editorial policy (some 90 percent endorsed Nixon-Agnew) they all have to draw their national and international news from the same single well, the national press corps.

Facts are hard things. But they must be faced. Like the big bands of the forties, the old journalism, where objectivity, balance and fairness were a trinity of values, is not coming back. College students switching by the hundreds into journalism courses are not signing up so that they might more faithfully record the events of their time. The Woodward-Bernstein generation is signing up because it wants to be on the cutting edge of social change. In the future, the gulf between a moderately conservative people and increasingly adversary press is certain to grow.

Big Business, which holds the purse strings and has the power to effect change, has all the enthusiasm for combat of the Royal Laotian Army. It tolerates the conspicuous anti-business bias of the networks, because the latter provides a national audience for business commercials. And that means more products sold, and higher profits all around. "Merchants have no country," Jefferson wrote. "The mere spot they stand on does not constitute so strong an attachment as that from which they draw their gains."[7] This father of the American Revolution had at least one sentiment in common with the father of the Russian Revolution. When the time comes to hang the capitalists, observed Lenin, they will be found bidding on the rope contract.

The FCC, like the school-yard bully, prefers to lift the licenses of fundamentalist preachers and Alabama segregationists, rather than mix it up with the big boys at the networks. If C.B.S. coverage of Vietnam and national security issues, as analyzed in the Lefever Report, is not a *prima facie* violation of the fairness doctrine, the doctrine is without meaning.

As for the Republican Administration, the issue of media bias has been jettisoned with every other vestige of its predecessor. The new White House will travel more than halfway to get along with everyone, even self-ordained adversaries. So Washington returns to normal; the scribes and pharisees hold dominion over all.

The Distribution of Wealth

I

In the spring of '72, the former Rhodes Scholar and political tactician who pieced together Mr. McGovern's delegate majority at Miami Beach sat in a Georgetown bar explaining patiently how the "demogrant" plan would make Richard Nixon a one-term President.

The theory ran thus: McGovern's program would mean added income for two-thirds of the nation, added taxes for one-third. When the two-thirds came to realize the Democrats had in mind pay hikes for them, at someone else's expense, they would handily outvote the one-third who would protest. And that would be the end of Mr. Nixon. As John Kennedy Galbraith summed it up: McGovern "will appeal to the unrich, unpowerful and unprivileged majority, and, therefore, he will be elected."[1]

Of itself, this $1,000 per-person scheme was adequate evidence to convince a majority of Americans that the Republicans were not just crying wolf when they warned that the South Dakota Democrat was the most radical candidate nominated by a major party in generations. The McGovern plan envisaged more than simply a guaranteed annual income of

$4000 for a family of four. It cut the tie between work and pay; it was designed to redistribute society's rewards, all along the line. Union workers who had done well at the bargaining table would be required to share their earnings with those who had not. The middle class and the wealthy were to make net transfers of income not only to those in need but to the working class as well. Under the program, everyone in America would be brought into the walfare system, and every man's income would be subject to readjustment, either up or down, toward a median pre-determined by George McGovern and his counselors.

Behind this profoundly radical scheme lay the conviction that a man's pay should no longer be determined by what his services would bring in the market place. Rather, government should intervene, with a positive duty to make more equal the rewards of society, regardless of individual merit or contribution. From each according to his ability, to each according to his need.

By late fall, with McGovern and Shriver running 30 lengths off the pace, the research assistant who had sold the Senator the package was being greeted around campaign headquarters with all the warmth and camaraderie co-workers might have mustered for a courtesy call from Charles Colson.

Mr. McGovern and his men terribly misread the nation. They underestimated working-class hostility toward welfare. They underestimated middle-class hostility toward new taxes, for whatever purpose. They saw a community of interest between the working and non-working poor, which the former themselves did not see. In 1972, the United States was unprepared for democratic socialism. Working- and middle-class Democrats, unlike the ideologically motivated intellectuals who control the party machinery and write its platform, care nothing for an "equality" which means they must drop a rung on the ladder of success, or share their rung with those below.

Senator McGovern, however, was not the only candidate in 1972 belatedly aware of the national animus against new taxes. For months, the President dallied with the idea of asking Congress for a $20 billion value-added tax. Only the public opinion surveys and the election returns of Governor Wallace's anti-tax campaign convinced the President and his domestic counselors to jettison the plan and emerge with a "no new taxes" commitment.

As the primaries and general election of '72 and the political rhetoric of '74 made manifest, the limits of taxpayer tolerance are being reached. No new social program can today compete in political appeal with tax relief, a development not without significance for the right, a development that has not gone unnoticed on the left. Herein may be found an issue— to succeed the "social issue"—on which to confront liberalism, and to bring about political realignment along the lines of the lost landslide of 1972.

But the Republican Party has been embarrassingly slow in recognizing the political potential of this development.

Last winter, the Democrats moved to preempt the issue. When President Ford proposed corporate tax relief and across-the-board personal tax cuts, to ease the burden on society's producers and to stimulate the economy, the Ninety-fourth Congress scrapped his plan, and substituted another.

They threw out the corporate tax reduction, added billions in new taxes on the oil industry and the multinational corporations, and proceeded to draft a "tax reform" measure which dropped millions off the tax rolls, and gave just about everyone in the country a $50, $100 or $200 check. The cost of the plan was enormous, running to almost $24 billion; but the stimulus it provided for the idle productive sector of the U.S. economy was almost nil.

It was a mockery of needed tax reform, another "income transfer" program drafted for the benefit of the Democratic Party, at the expense of the middle class; and President Ford made one of the worst mistakes of his Presidency in not vetoing the measure and drawing a clear line between what he stood for, and what the national Democrats proposed.

The Democrats' plan could have been pulled straight out of a socialist textbook on how to use the tax code to redistribute the wealth; the Republicans, however, had no alternative philosophy to fall back upon, and publicly defend. Their response to the Democratic coup was to try to extract a few crumbs, some face-saving amendments, and claim partial credit from the beneficiaries.

II

Common sense, as well as the experience of the seventies, argues aloud that if there is any future for the right in politics, it is to echo and articulate the voice of the working and middle class, not the welfare class. As Mr. Nixon's years demonstrated, there is no future in that other direction.

More than once, the former President sought to steal a march on his liberal adversaries, to turn the left flank of the Democratic Party. In August of 1969, the candidate elected to office denouncing the guaranteed annual income startled Congress, and not least its conservative wing, with a Family Assistance Plan, guaranteeing to every family $2,400 in cash income. The proposal caught the national press and Democratic party flat-footed. They were suitably impressed, but they were not immobilized.

Not to be outdone in generosity, the Democrats had within months devised and introduced welfare plans of their own, the presentation of which, at regular intervals, made Mr. Nixon's once radical plan appear increasingly conservative. As the President held to $2,400, the cost of poker went up, until the black caucus drove everyone out of the game recommending a $6500 guaranteed annual income for everyone in the United States.

What was dramatic in August of 1969 seemed downright stingy by January of 1972. And the President's refusal to raise his original $2,400—coupled with a dog-in-the-manger attitude of Democratic liberals who preferred no reform to a "Nixon reform"—finally convinced the Ninety-second Congress to reject FAP as just another miserly little Republican program which "failed utterly to meet the real needs of the people." And so it goes.

No Republican President can successfully flank the Democratic Party on the left. For Republicans to attempt such a strategy is simply to move the center of American politics continually leftward. Consider. The Republican Administration took the lead in proposing an increase in the minimum wage to $2 an hour; the Democrats insisted that $2.30 was the very floor of decency. Mr. Nixon proposed a national health insurance scheme—a radical departure for a Republican. Mr. Kennedy countered with one twice as large, twice as costly. The Republican proposed that the elderly on Social Security receive a 5 percent increase in annual benefits; the Democrats demanded and got 20 percent.

Republicans are caught up in a three-cornered game for which the Democrats and the press have written the rules. So long as the plaudits and publicity go to politicians who "care" more, because they spend more, traditional Republicans cannot but come off as less concerned, less generous, less humane.

Consider. Among the clichés of the national press is that under Nelson Rockefeller's regime, "New York was the best-governed state in the nation." Over and over one may hear it repeated. The American Political Science Association confirmed as much in an official study. But, by whose standards is this so?

Certainly, not by conservative standards. Nor by Republican standards Nor by the standards of the voters of New York, who in recent political surveys, named the former governor as the least popular major politician in the state. His hand-picked successor, who struggled unsuccessfully to free himself of the Rockefeller connection, drowned in a sea of hostile votes.

Why there remains a residue of dissatisfaction with the governor, where he ruled rather than where he currently resides, is not difficult to understand. As *Barron's* editorialized in the fall of 1974:

> Under Rockefeller, taxes were imposed or increased at least every other year: in 1959, 1963, 1965, 1966, 1968, 1969, 1971 and 1972. During Rocky's tenure in office,

the maximum rate on the personal income tax more than doubled from 7% to 15% . . . the state gasoline levy advanced from four to eight cents a gallon, the cigaret tax from three to 15 cents a pack. A 4% state sales tax went on the books. All told, in 15 years, the tax load had nearly quintupled, to the point where, according to the Citizens Public Expenditure Survey, Inc., taxpayers in New York State are the most over burdened in the land.[2]

With the tax bite more painful each year, many business firms and citizens pulled up stakes and moved on. During the Rockefeller era in Albany, California replaced New York as the nation's most populous state. In 1971 and 1972, the Empire State actually lost population; some 120,000 moved away. In the state capital, a select committee found that, in the governor's years, New York suffered a major decline in manufacturing, and a loss of job opportunities. Among the reasons given was that business perceived, not inaccurately, an anti-business climate.

Again the question: by whose standards was New York, under Nelson Rockefeller, the "best-governed state in the nation?" Only if one accepts the esoteric and unrepresentative standards of liberal professors and national press can one concur in such an assessment.

For years in this country—and even today—political observers have tended to judge the quality of government in a city or state by the level of per capita public expenditures for health and education. By that yardstick New York City and New York State invariably stood at or near the top. But the hundreds of thousands who have fled that city, and the thousands still annually fleeing the state, testify eloquently that this country has been using an utterly false standard of judgment.

Perhaps we should rank communities by how people vote with their feet. And by that standard New Hampshire, with no sales tax, no income tax, and with immigrants pouring in from all over New England, should be adjudged among the "best-governed states in the nation."

But to suggest that Governor Thompson and his predecessors in New Hampshire have been successful chief executives while Nelson Rockefeller was a manifest failure is, in this city, to commit a political atrocity.

Conservative and traditional Republicans confront a dilemma. The modern journalist and the historian's "ideal" of an executive corresponds closely to the "ideal" of the Democratic Party. If a Republican governor following conservative principles runs a surplus, reduces taxes and creates a climate which attracts investment, business and jobs, his achievements will be ignored in fulsome praise of the governor who raises taxes, funds new social programs, runs a deficit and drives business out of the state.

Similar standards are applied to legislators. The Republican senators who conform most closely to the press' "ideal" receive the most regular and favorable publicity, i.e. Weicker, Schweicker, Percy and Brooke. The volume and character of press coverage a national Republican receives is directly proportional to the distance he travels away from his party's conservative point of view.

Awareness of this reality by Republican senators and presidents is a primary magnet drawing so many leeward once they attain office. Perhaps it will ever be thus. Gerald Ford, a regular Republican in the House, was not in the Oval Office a week before aides were assuring the White House press that his previous voting record reflected his Grand Rapids constituency, not his convictions, and certainly not his future course.

While an increasingly conservative electorate puts men into office, an increasingly liberal press alone can append to a politician's name, in time and eternity, the appelation "great." Thus, running for office, politicians listen to their constituency; in office, to the press.

III

The last best hope of the Republican Party to regain its lost primacy is to part company with the press and place itself at the head of the middle-class revolution boiling in the countryside. Through history the "distribution of wealth" has been an issue over which revolutions have been ignited and wars fought. It can become the issue on which to bring about a realignment of parties.

The hour is late indeed. Through the acquiescence, indeed the active collaboration of Republicans, the United States is fast approaching a point where a critical number of citizens will be almost wholly dependent upon government for their basic needs.

There are today 5.6 million Americans getting unemployment benefits, 11 million on welfare, almost 17 million employed by the federal, state and local governments, and the armed services, another 20 million on food stamps, and almost 31 million living off Social Security.

The effect upon the American economy of this growing phenomenon is becoming as serious as upon the nation's political process. Surveying the situation in January of 1975, *The Wall Street Journal* found:

> As recently as 1965, government transfer payments to individuals came to a modest $37.1 billion. Last month, federal, state and local governments were disbursing cash to individuals at an annual rate of $155.9 billion, for which no services are rendered. These include Social Security pensions, government pensions of all kinds, unemployment benefits, black-lung money, food stamps, welfare payments and health insurance benefits. While the payments are of course defended on grounds of compassion, they are having a serious effect on the economy, by steadily breaking down the relationship between reward and effort.[3]

Though no voting bloc is irretrievably lost, the expanding army of government employees and government dependents represents a natural constituency of the Democratic Party. No Republican can remain true to party principle and compete with what the Democrats are willing to promise and deliver to these voters.

If there is a role for the Republican Party, it is to be the party of the working class, not the welfare class. It is to champion the cause of producers and taxpayers, of the private sector threatened by the government sector, of the millions who carry most of the cost of government and share least in its beneficence. To the degree that Republicans echo the conventional wisdom about government being the indispensable engine of social progress we testify to our obsolescence. We dig our own graves.

For what has government accomplished with fifteen years of relentless federal activism. Certainly, on one side of the ledger, there has been marked improvement in the living standards of those on relief, and on federal pensions. But an irretrievable social price has been paid. Literally millions of Americans have been permanently transformed from independent citizens of the Republic into wards of the state. And much of the private wealth upon which the future prosperity of society depends has been drained off by politicians to be spent and consumed here and now.

Nor has the extraordinary generosity of taxpayers produced any perceptible sense of gratitude on the part of the poor, or of the intelligentsia which promised us social peace if we enacted these reforms. The more the welfare state blossoms and grows, the louder its advocates and beneficiaries denounce the rest of society as cruel, heartless and corrupt. What was it the Austrian statesman said after marching out of the Congress of Vienna with the most favorable of terms, "We will astonish the world with our ingratitude."

Having invested tens of billions of dollars in foreign aid to unknown lands, and hundreds of billions for the less fortunate in our own country, Americans have truly come to know the truth of the statement: never do a man a favor, he will never forgive you. Gratitude, Carl Hayden once explained, is an emotion folks feel in anticipation of good things yet to come.

A quarter-century ago, a young House Democrat declared in the Congress that "Every time we try to lift a problem from our own shoulders, and shift that problem to the hands of the government, to the same extent we are sacrificing the liberties of our people."[4] To those who share the sentiment and concern of Congressman John F. Kennedy of Massachusetts, Republicans must appeal. The redistribution of wealth, away from government, its workers, wards and dependents, back to the individuals and institutions which produced it, is an issue about which Republicans might yet gather a majority.

IV

The Republicans' preferred vehicle for returning "power to the people" has been the much-touted general revenue sharing, legislative altar piece of the Nixon years, under which the Federal Government, with few strings, annually distributes $6 billion to state and local governments. As originally envisioned, revenue sharing would have replaced federal social programs. As enacted, revenue sharing has simply been added to the list. While a traditional favorite of mayors and governors who spend the money, the program and the attendant propaganda about restoring power to the people are clear violations of truth in advertising.

Contrary to the claims, general revenue sharing does not reduce the size or cost of government; it enlarges the federal tax take. It expands local and state government where growth has been greatest these past twenty years. It does not return funds to the taxpayers; it merely transfers funds from one government which runs regular deficits to other governments, state and local, which generally run in the black. It allows hundreds of politicians across the nation to indulge in the politically irresponsible practice of spending tax dollars they did not raise themselves.

Thus far, some $20 billion has been dispatched by Democratic Congresses to be spent at the discretion of dominantly Democratic mayors and governors; and Republicans catalogue this among their proudest achievements. As P. T. Barnum said, there is a Republican born every minute and two Democrats there to receive him.

V

Of the congressional Democrats, it can be said, they take care of their own. No tax reform is allowed passage which is not first reshaped to conform with their redistribute-the-wealth philosophy. Whatever the measure proposed, a rake-off is included for their own constituencies.

Republicans, however, seem either embarrassed or unwilling to represent the interests of their natural constituency, those who provide the benefits rather than those who receive them. As a consequence, the interests of the productive sector of society, which are often coterminus with the national interest, too often go unrepresented and undefended.

The Republican Party is currently undergoing an identity crisis, deciding what it is, and for whom it shall speak. And if it will not voice the concerns of the neglected majority, some other entity is needed.

Rarely, if ever, has the Republican Party advanced a broad tax reform program thoroughly consistent with both its conservative philosophy and political interests. President Ford's proposal conceded too much at the outset to Democratic philosophy; and before the plan became law, he was forced to concede almost everything.

Among the guidelines of Republican tax reform should be these: 1) The private sector, which produces the nation's wealth, should be left with a significantly larger percentage of the nation's resources, and government, basically non-productive, should be left with less. 2) Savings and investment should be favored over consumption. 3) Reform should be tailored to make American business and industry more competitive in the world's markets, and to promote long-term growth. 4) Lastly, for reasons economic, political and practi-

cal, it should not discriminate against society's most successful.

One such reform was advanced in the Ninety-third Congress by former Colorado Congressman Donald Brotzman. A
simple proposal, it would make the first $1,000 in interest in-
come, which a couple earns on its savings account, non-tax-
able. Thus, $20,000 put into a savings and loan at 5 percent
would earn annually $1000 in tax-free income. The measure
would benefit those who save, not those who spend. It would
help protect savings against inflation. It would transfer income from government back to those who earned it. It would
benefit primarily not the rich to whom the tax saving would
be insignificant, but the middle class. Finally, it would encourage the accumulation of capital, a national necessity. Over
the last decade, the United States rate of capital accumulation
—which has a direct bearing on the growth of productivity
and hence upon inflation—has been less than 20 percent, about
the same as Great Britain. In France, it has been 25 percent,
in Germany 26 percent, in Japan 33 percent.

A second proposal is reduction of the top rate of taxation
on individual income, now 70 percent, to a level roughly
twice that of the bottom rate of 14 percent—i.e. setting the
maximum federal tax take at 30 percent of personal income.
No economic or social goal worth attaining justifies this in-
herently unfair confiscatory tax, imposed upon society's most
successful members.

Because of this steeply progressive and foolish feature of
the federal tax, millions of man-hours of the most able of
American citizens are annually set aside searching for tax
shelters to protect income which by right is already theirs.

There is only one logical explanation why the U.S. thus
apes some European governments in the level of taxation on
personal income. That explanation may be found in Churchill's characterization of socialism as "the greed of ignorance
and the gospel of envy."

Certainly, there is no economic justification for this rank
discrimination against the well-to-do. Only a small fraction
of federal revenues comes from rates above 30 percent.

Assuredly, any Republican candidate or President who proposed such a reform would be damned for selling out to the rich. But so what. Are we not already so condemned? And who would suffer terribly from such a proposal? Would the poor and lowest income who pay no federal income taxes take to the barricades because their benefactors are only being required to turn three of every ten dollars they earn over to the Federal Government? A fifth of the American people earn more than $20,000 a year; 5 percent earn more than $30,000. One wonders what injustice these people have committed that we should constantly devise ways and means to deprive them of ever-increasing shares of what they have earned.

The only institution that could feel a genuine sense of loss at this reform would be the Treasury of the United States.

Today, the 30 percent tax rate cuts in, for single taxpayers, at $14,000 in net income—for married taxpayers at $20,000. Everyone above these figures, literally millions, would benefit. The nation, too, would benefit because more of its wealth was being left in the hands of individuals who buy the big ticket items, who place a significant share of their earnings in investment and savings. Millions of the most able and successful of our citizens might applaud a politician and party that would take such a stand in the face of today's ceaseless demagoguery against the successful. And if the Democratic Party wished to fight the proposition to the death, let them take the consequences of baiting the middle class.

The politicians and ideologues who seek to use the tax code to gain power for government and level society are not voting Republican in any event. Their opposition, their hostility, is not something that should be compromised, but something that should be courted. They are lost to the Republican Party; and no concession need be made to win their approval.

As William F. Buckley, Jr. argues in *Four Reforms*, the ideal in a democratic society should be equality of sacrifice by citizens equal in rights, i.e. a flat proportionate rate on all incomes, from which no one is exempt. That is the direction in which conservatives should move. After all, it was, if one recalls correctly, Karl Marx who insisted in his *Communist Manifesto* upon "a heavy progressive or graduated income tax," the purpose of which was to expropriate the men of wealth. That is not what the United States is, or should be, about.

"To tax the community for the advantage of a class is not protection. It is plunder." So said Disraeli a century ago. To-day the tax burden on the productive community is enormous. And the lower-income class has been, in ten years, relieved of federal taxes and provided with federal benefits ranging from medicare to medicaid, food stamps and social security increases far in excess of the cost of living, large increments in welfare, housing subsidies, legal services, VISTA volunteers, OEO, Job Corps, scholarships and social services. Enough is enough. If the depredations of the middle class by Robin Hood on behalf of the "poor" are endless and excessive, it will not be long before a majority rallies behind the Sheriff of Nottingham.

VI

But if the 70 percent tax on personal income is a testament to greed, the 48 percent tax which the U.S. imposes upon business income is a monument to folly. Forgotten in the neo-populist claptrap about cracking down on the obscene profits of the big boys is just who it is who pays the corporate tax.

It is not Henry Ford II or Mr. Gerstenberg who pay the corporate tax for the Ford Motor Company and General Motors. Their salaries, like those of other corporate officers, are customarily set well before the end of the fiscal year. As is apparent now, such men suffer a good deal less than auto workers when inventories are high and profits down. Those who actually pay the corporate tax for Ford and GM are the tens of thousands who buy Fords and Chevrolets. To a giant corporation, the income tax, like rent expense, is another cost of doing business, to be factored into the price of the product. Corporations are less taxpayers than tax collectors. As always, the consumer pays the bill.

Indeed, if corporate taxes do not come from the consumer, they must come either out of potential dividends of stockholders or past earnings. Which means they will be paid for in future investment and jobs.

In taxing corporate profits at 48 percent—a higher rate than in Germany and Japan—the Government has allowed the anti-business sentiments and attitudes carried over from the Depression to jeopardize the interests of the country, the consumer, the taxpayer, and the job-seeker alike. It has placed American enterprise at a competitive disadvantage with the rest of the world. For what?

Corporate profits are the seed corn of the economy. They not only provide the country with investment capital; when high they attract other investment capital. And a government that consumes, as ours does, almost half the corporate profits in the system, is a government inadvertently stunting its economic growth.

Within the country today, there appears a widespread growing ignorance of both the level and the role of profits in our economic system. Not infrequently, in supposedly sophisticated quarters, one can hear expressed a passionate hostility to the very idea of profit. Fault for this must rest with the economics departments of our colleges, the business community and the press.

For over twenty years, since 1951, business profits have been declining as a percentage of personal and national income. The average for a U.S. company has been running between 4 and 5 percent of sales, too low to guarantee the steady flow of investment capital without which there can be no sustained economic growth. Yet, a survey not long ago found that the average American believed corporate profits were running at 28 percent of sales, some five times higher than the actual rate.

Why this is so is not difficult to understand.

On 23 October 1974, Mr. Walter Cronkite reported to his CBS audience of millions a startling 1,200 percent increase in the third-quarter profits of the Great Western United Corporation, parent of Great Western Sugar Corporation, over 1973. To any housewife who had recently returned from the market where sugar prices had soared, sentiment about Great Western would have been something less than cordial.

But it would have been the truth, and a good deal more informative if less polarizing, had Mr. Cronkite stated that: "Today, Great Western United Corporation reported a profit of 11 percent on sales of $180 million in the third quarter, a considerable improvement over the third quarter of 1973, when Great Western recorded profits of less than 2 percent on sales of only $91 million." The constant comparison of profit-to-profit, rather than the more significant profit-to-sales, has left the country with a grossly distorted portrait of corporate prosperity.

The next evening Mr. Cronkite reported that General Motors' profits dropped 94 percent in the third quarter of 1974. Knowing only this fact, it is possible to predict that should General Motors' profits in the third quarter of 1975 return to only half of what they were in the third quarter of 1973, Mr. Cronkite will be able accurately to report an 800 percent increase in GM profits over '74.

The anti-business sentiment in the country might diminish somewhat if the networks and business community jointly conspired to tell the truth: that profits as a percentage of national income have fallen for a quarter century, that they average less than 5 percent of sales, that if they do not increase in the future our traditional prosperity must become a thing of the past. Business' desire to paint its profit picture in the most brilliant of colors is as congenital as the networks' desire to dramatize the dullest news. But headline grabbing by both has left the nation with the false impression that business has prospered at the public expense.

VII

Even though rejected in Congress, President Ford's request of Congress that government reduce its take of corporate profits from 48 percent to 42 percent was both courageous and overdue. Ideally, because corporate taxes mean higher prices for consumers, fewer dividends for investors, or reduced investment capital for expansion and jobs, the corporate tax is a regressive tax that should be eliminated altogether. In the current political climate, however, that is out of the question. And in the current climate, President Ford took a significant step.

Given the unpopularity of big business, the complexity of the economy, and the widespread ignorance of how the system works, the corporate tax is an issue that lends itself to demagoguery. It can be framed in the most simplistic and deceptive terms: "should the working man be forced to pay for these reforms, or should the rich powerful corporations?" Using variations on the theme, politicians have fastened upon business and industry new taxes, rules and regulations that have called into question the long-term survivability of the system. We need only look across the Atlantic to the British Isles to see the future, and how it works. The greater the government intervention in an economy, it seems a general rule for the world, developed and underdeveloped, the less free the people, the less prosperous the society. This most successful of capitalist societies would be well advised to set as its goal a federal tax upon business that was—unlike today—the lowest in the industrial world. It would be well advised to restructure the tax code for individuals and corporations to favor, rather than penalize, capital formation.

Beyond the board room perhaps, tax cuts for corporations is an unpopular position. But it has the advantage of being the right position. President Kennedy acted upon that recognition with the successful investment tax credit of 1962. Lyndon Johnson did so with the tax reform of 1964. And President Ford should stick to his guns.

Republicans, sensitive to the allegation that theirs is the party of business, have been reluctant to champion the interests of business. Understandably so. But the question being decided now is a fundamental one; it cannot be finessed. Will it be private enterprise, responsive to the individual and the market, or government, responsive to its prevailing ideology, that controls and disburses the investment capital of society; and hence that decides what kind of nation we shall become?

The corporate income tax is but another front of the great conflict between the men of private enterprise and the men of government for control of the nation's wealth, its economy and its destiny. The national Democrats have taken their stand—with government. The Republican Party, however, the party of private enterprise, is waffling on its principles, and compromising its convictions. And if the free enterprise system is exchanged for the inferior models we are being offered, it will not be because the system has failed but because its defenders and beneficiaries have failed. As the late philosopher Richard Weaver wrote, "many traditional positions in our world have suffered not so much because of inherent defect as because of the stupidity, ineptness and intellectual sloth of those who . . . are presumed to have their defense in charge."[5]

VIII

There are several other reforms which should commend themselves to those concerned about the bias in the U.S. tax against capital formation and in favor of consumption. The first would be a steep increase in the current $50,000 ceiling of the corporate profits of small business which are taxed at the lower 22 percent. The private sector would benefit; small business, long a bulwark of the Republican Party, would be assisted; and more investment capital would be left where it belongs and will do society the greatest good.

A second reform is a reduction in the federal tax on capital gains. At its present level this tax is a deterrent to commerce, and a disincentive to capital investment. In Israel a small socialist country which recognizes the need of sustained economic activity, there is no capital gains tax. Reduction here would provide a noninflationary shot of adrenalin to the economy and a booster shot to the stock market.

A third proposal was advanced last October 9 in the pages of *The Wall Street Journal* by Hofstra Professor Leo Barnes. It is an old idea with modern merit. That is for government to end the double-taxation of dividends. Currently, income used in paying dividends to stockholders is taxed first as corporate profits, and, secondly, as personal income to the stockholder. Professor Barnes argues that, for both accounting and tax purposes, dividends be considered a corporate expense, and hence deductible.[6]

Just as interest, which is deductible as an expense, is the cost of raising money through borrowing and bond issues, so dividends are the cost of raising money in the stock market.

While this reform might stimulate higher dividend payments, and surely lower corporate taxes, there would be a partial pick-up by government at the other end—in the individual tax returns of shareholders. More important, such a reform would provide business with a magnet for capital investment; and it would turn the market instantly into a bull.

Among the considerations behind the foregoing is that each leaves a larger share of business profits in business hands. Which is as it should be, for reasons economic and political, pragmatic and philosophic.

Like it or not, we are the leading capitalist power on earth, a planet where, as a general rule, the less capitalist the country the less prosperous the people. We have nothing to be defensive about. In the economic systems of other societies there is little to emulate or envy and a great deal we ought religiously to avoid. The United States was built by men and women who turned their backs upon Europe. And in watching the management of Europe's political and economic affairs since, one finds little reason to doubt that original judgment. Our ambition should not be to ape the social welfare states of Western Europe, but to hold out an alternative, to set an example for the world. National security is the only argument why America's income taxes should not be the lowest in the world, her business the freest, and her markets as open to goods as we want them open to ideas. Government should focus its attention upon the neediest, guaranteeing that those who cannot care for themselves are cared for. Beyond providing a floor of dignity under each of its citizens, government should cease to concern itself with rearranging the rewards of society, which are not its business.

Government's record over the last sixth of a century argues aloud that politicians not be entrusted with more power, or more of the nation's wealth. The institutions government runs, the Post Office and the public schools, are among our least efficient and least successful. And government's management of the economy—the hundreds of billions in deficits, the shortages and dislocations caused by wage and price controls, the double-digit inflation, the interest rates pushed to the ceiling by government borrowing, the subsequent recession—provide unrebutted testimony against further intervention.

IX

No reform of the internal revenue code, however, should be completed without Congressional scrutiny of the political and social impact of 501(C)3—the loophole dealing with tax-exempt organizations.

Originally, tax exemptions were granted to encourage private giving to religious, charitable and educational institutions. Over the last generation, however, the number of exempt organizations has proliferated. Their population, only 1,000 in 1950, is now in the tens of thousands; their assets are in the billions, and their activities range far beyond the narrow perimeters originally envisioned in the law.

Consider the most powerful and most publicized of such institutions, the Ford Foundation, established in the thirties by the Sage of Dearborn to evade inheritance taxes on the stock of the Ford Motor Company. Before the market slump, the Ford Foundation boasted resources roughly equal to those of its nine closest rivals, taken together. Depending upon the vicissitudes of Dow-Jones, Ford's assets range between 2 and

4 billion dollars; its annual grants, until recently, have run in excess of $200 million.

Prior to the arrival of Mr. Nixon in Washington, the Ford Foundation was literally running amok beyond the guidelines set down by the law for tax-free foundations.

Ford "grants" went to eight of Robert Kennedy's campaign staffers for "travel and study," and one $13,000 grant went to LBJ's domestic counselor, Joseph Califano, for seven weeks of effort to write a piece on student disorders. When the CIA, after some unfortunate publicity, ceased funding the leftist National Student Association, the Ford Foundation stepped into the breach. Radical Mexican-American organizations in the Southwest got Ford money, as did a voter registration drive in Cleveland, which helped to elect a Democratic Mayor. And that harlequinade on the Mall, Resurrection City, featuring Ralph David Abernathy as ringmaster, might never have taken place had it not been for a timely Ford advance of a quarter million dollars to the Southern Christian Leadership Conference, the sponsoring organization.

Then, there was the Ford financial backing for the ill-fated Ocean Hill-Brownsville school decentralization project in New York City, which produced a city-wide teachers' strike and, in the words of one Pulitzer-prize winning reporter, as "jarring, bitter and vicious, a confrontation as New York has experienced . . . , which exacerbated existing differences in New York especially between blacks and Jews."

As Albert Shanker, leader of the teachers union, assessed it, "They (the Ford people) feel we're on the verge of guerrilla warfare and the only chance is to make a deal with the guerrillas. So Ford subsidizes the revolutionaries and puts them on the payroll which makes being a revolutionary a hell of a lot easier."[7]

Motivated partially by the above record of Ford and the perceived hubris of executive officer, McGeorge Bundy, whose commission conceived the school decentralization project, Congress in 1969 acted. Tighter restrictions on activities were approved. A 4 percent excise tax on foundation income was imposed. Foundations were required to disburse, annually by 1975, 6 percent of their equity—to prevent limitless growth. This is all history. Subsequent to 1969, both Ford and Bundy have maintained what is termed a low profile. Nevertheless, Ford's current activities raise as many political questions as its past.

Among them is the Ma Bell-Western Electric relationship Mr. Bundy and Ford have established with Washington's Brookings Institution. This latter has become, in effect, the issues and research arm of the liberal wing of the Democratic Party; and it provided, for liberal bureaucrats fleeing Mr. Nixon's government, the same sanctuary the medieval church provided for escaping felons. Over the past decade, Ford has given Brookings funds estimated in the tens of millions.

The question raised here is the one addressed in the campaign reform act of 1974—the influence of big money in politics. Congressional Democrats maneuvered through the Ninety-third Congress legislation to curtail severely and permanently the traditional Republican advantage in big givers in election years. Some of those Republican funds, however, were spent on hiring the kind of writing and research talent that Brookings keeps on tap, free of charge, for the national Democrats.

Nor is Brookings the only such institution carried by Ford. There is likely not a major liberal or left-wing political affairs or public policy institute that has not been on the receiving end of a Ford grant. Many of these institutes are little more than halfway houses for the intellectuals, bureaucrats and politicians dreaming of and working for the restoration to power of the Kennedy wing of the Democratic Party.

Republicans and conservatives have no tax-exempt exchequer that can approach Ford in aggressiveness and assets. Indeed, if the political right, rather than the left, had captured the empire of Henry Ford I, one may be sure there would be legislation sailing through Congress today, to correct the unfair imbalance of the political process against the left. Republicans or conservatives have no reason to acquiesce forever in the ongoing employment of the Ford billions in behalf of what Daniel Patrick Moynihan has accurately described as the "political agenda of a fairly small group of intellectuals."

If, as we are constantly reminded, Mr. Liddy threatened the nation's political system on a budget of a quarter million; if, as we have been told, the CIA was able to "destabilize" the Chilean economy on a budget of $8 million—then, assuredly, the $200 million in tax-free funds Ford annually distributes to its favorites can upset the political balance and distort the political process in the United States.

Among the recent beneficiaries of Ford gifts have been "public interest law firms," those latest immigrants to step ashore in the teeming new world of tax exemption. In the name of the environment, consumer protection, social justice and the poor, these firms have marched into half the federal courts of the country to force increases in government spending, to block business expansion, to frustrate change with which they disagree.

Though they claim to represent the "public interest," they represent only their own ideology. They are among the nation's new unelected elite determining the course of this country.

Was it truly "in the public interest" to have tied up the Alaskan pipeline in the courts for years? Is it truly in the public interest to block off-shore drilling and the building of nuclear power plants which might stave off a depression and make the United States self-sufficient in energy?

Without the Ford funds, without their tax exemption, these attorneys and their allies would be required to compete in the social and political arena on the same basis as the rest of the nation.

The Ford Foundation is an empire and a law unto itself. There is no public participation in the selection of Ford trustees, no public influence over the decisions of Ford executives, no public accounting by Ford's management. Mr. Bundy was chosen by its board of directors, a self-perpetuating body that nominates in secret ballot to fill its own vacancies. Where the businessman answers in the marketplace, where the elected politician answers at the polls, the Ford Foundation answers to no one. Not unexpectedly, the new Congress seems to have lost interest in the subject. Late last fall, Mr. Bundy was heard to observe, "I sense a growing feeling in Washington that they see a 6 percent payout and the 4 percent net investment tax as excessive."[8]

With new and sympathetic ears on Capitol Hill, the Ford Foundation, which pays an income tax one-twelfth the rate of the Ford Motor Company, may be in line for tax relief.

It was an imbalance in the private wealth available to Republican presidential candidates that persuaded the Democratic Congress to restrict campaign contributions and equalize expenditures. Similarly, the use of the Ford billions to advance social causes favored by the left, the use of its satellite institutions as tax-free sanctuaries for liberal scholars, researchers, bureaucrats and politicians, should produce legislation from the right.

In the absence of a more representative board and senior staff at the nation's most powerful foundation, and a more proportionate pattern of giving that does not discriminate so manifestly against conservatives—the right should make it a subject of legislative policy to effect the dismantling of the Ford Foundation.

X

Yet, breaking down the Ford Foundation, though desirable in and of itself, does not address the large question.

The larger question arises from the fact that it is no longer the original purpose of the tax exemption—to promote religious, educational and charitable enterprises—that is being served by the hundreds of organizations slipping annually through this enormous loophole in the U.S. tax code. Increasingly, it is the social and political agenda—and occasionally the personal fortunes—of powerful men like the Rockefellers, their retainers and the intellectuals at the apex of the Ford

Foundation that is being advanced by these tax-free dollars subsidized by the American middle class.

The tens of millions in grants such foundations, along with the public policy institutes, dispense annually for studies, reports, research projects are basically outright subsidies to sustain a whole privileged class of verbalists they wish to keep "on tap"—many of whom contribute a good deal less to the national well-being than the average plumber or carpenter.

This whole invisible empire, and its impact, upon the nation's political life, is an issue that needs to be put on the front burner.

Is there any reason such activity should be exempt at all from the normal taxation imposed upon other institutions? Why should the very rich be allowed to deduct from their income, for tax purposes, the thousands they pour into such adventures? If the U.S. taxpayer must subsidize with higher taxes the decisions of the Ford and Rockefeller Foundations, should he not have a hand in the selection of the men who make those decisions?

How consistent is it with the basic principles of American democracy for these vast concentrations of inherited wealth to escape taxation and be put at the perpetual disposal of a chosen elite, which lives off those fortunes, even as it employs those huge resources to play social engineer and patron of the arts?

In any event no better occasion will arise to debate these matters than the Bicentennial Year of 1976, when the taxpayers revolt intersects with the presidential election.

☆

Economic and Social Policy

I

The bicentennial year of American independence, 1976, is the bicentennial as well of publication of *The Wealth of Nations*. Adam Smith's classic is to the capitalist West what Marx' *Das Kapital* is to the Communist East; and the two-hundredth anniversary of its appearance will be a fateful year for capitalism.

In the closing days of 1974, the economist Otto Eckstein, surveying the nation's economic situation, declared, "We either work our way out of this mess in 1975 or we are in real trouble . . . if policy does not meet the challenge next year, we'll have to change the economic system."[1]

Given the policies being pursued by Congress and the Executive, the nation will not, by 1976, have emerged from the swamp into which the fiscal and monetary policies of a decade have plunged the American people. And, unless countervailing arguments and political forces are set in motion, the direction in which the nation shall then proceed is not difficult to predict.

In any free economy, there is a meridian which government cannot cross without the economy ceasing to be free. It is difficult to identify with precision where that meridian is located. But, clearly, Great Britain has crossed over that line, and the United States is approaching.

U.S. corporate and capital gains taxes are among the highest in the industrial world. Health, safety, consumer and environmental regulations imposed upon industry consume an ever increasing share of the nation's investment capital. One in every five working Americans is now on a government payroll. Almost 50 million citizens now depend, as their primary source of income, upon a regular government check. A third of the nation's GNP passes annually through the hands of government.

The private sector, saddled with regulations and controls, with a growing share of available investment capital diverted to taxes and to nonproductive requirements, is less and less capable of pulling the country out of the ditch into which the policies of government have pushed us. By the default of some and the design of others, before the decade's end, we may well have changed the system under which we live. And that would be an historic tragedy, of our own making.

II

The economic decisions that put us hip-deep in the Big Muddy are not difficult to trace.

In the middle sixties, President Johnson declared the nation could finance, on an installment plan, both a land war in Asia and his Great Society at home. The last full fiscal year of Lyndon Johnson left the U.S. with the largest deficit, $25 billion, since World War II. This deficit sharply accelerated the inflation already moving through the economy when Mr. Nixon took the oath of office. The mildly restrictive economic policies set in motion by the Republicans cooled the economy producing the mini-recession of 1970, which in turn prevented Republican political gains in the off-year. After that experience economics took a back seat to politics at the White House. Anxious not to enter a presidential year with the economy running at less than breakneck speed, the Republicans in 1971 and 1972 opened the sluices and the dollars flowed. Back-to-back $23 billion deficits were run in the two years preceding the election of 1972. To control unpleasant side effects, such as a rising consumer price index, the GOP went down to the Democratic barn and stole the bridle of wage-and-price controls.

Reviewing the election returns of November 1972, the stratagem was not unsuccessful—politically. The controls, however, created predictable distortions and shortages. When removed, the suppressed inflation broke forth with a vengeance, consuming at a double-digit rate the savings, income, pensions, insurance and confidence of a whole nation.

Aghast at the worst inflation in generations, the Administration moved toward austerity; and the politicians shuffled rapidly toward the right. Everyone, it seemed, in the off-year elections of 1974 ran as a "fiscal conservative." When the election passed, however, it was evident that the restrictive policies were working—only too well. Inflation was beginning to ease, but unemployment was rising rapidly, and the nation was suddenly deep in a major recession. The fiscal conservatives of October became the big spenders of January, demanding budget deficits of $70 billion through combined tax reduction and spending increases.

In the final days of 1974, Alan Greenspan warned that if this nation would not now take its medicine, and accept the price of breaking out of this inflationary spiral, we might not cure it for twenty years. But nobody was listening. Battling recession with tax cuts and social spending is more pleasant and profitable at election time than fighting inflation. By mid-January, the Administration and Congress were in spirited competition over who could be more generous to the taxpayers. As anticipated, the Congress prevailed with a $24 billion tax cut, and a proposed $68 billion deficit. Come the fall of 1976, we shall, therefore, be in the Year of the Scapegoat. The country will want to know who was responsible for the unemployment and the prices rising again. The Republicans will blame the Democrats who have controlled both Houses of Congress for twenty-two years. And the Democrats will blame the Republicans who have controlled the White House for eight. Both will be right.

The painful situation in which the United States finds itself is caused largely by a lack of courage and vision, and an abundance of irresponsibility, in both parties. Under five Democratic Congresses, and Presidents Johnson, Nixon and Ford, the U.S. Government will by mid-1976 have spent some $225 billion more than it collected in revenues. To finance this decade-long binge, government shouldered its way into the capital markets, drove up interest rates, and soaked up the investment dollars the nation's enterprises and industries needed for expansion and orderly growth. And government increased the supply of money at an annual rate well in excess of the growth of productivity, guaranteeing inflation.

The vicious cycle cannot continue indefinitely. As the economy lurches back and forth, from deficits and inflation, to unemployment and recession, each swing becomes wider, each trough deeper. The country is behaving like an addict. As soon as it comes down off a high with fever and chills, it swears off the stuff forever. But when the agonies of withdrawal set in, it demands louder and louder—and gets from the politicians—a quick fix to ease the pain.

But there are only two alternatives to cold turkey. One is a lifetime on methadone, and the other is death.

III

Come 1976, the politicians whose votes in Congress created the inflation which in turn brought on recession, will, like the Walrus and the Carpenter, be weeping over the victims.

Neither government, nor the politicians, however, will be cast as the villain of the piece. Rather, we shall hear ceaseless demagogy about the "windfall profits" of oil cartels, about avaricious sheiks in the Middle East and famine in the sub-

continent, about middlemen, corporate greed and price goug-
ers of a thousand varieties. Even these hardy perennials, the
gnomes of Zurich, will not escape without twenty lashes well
laid on.

And the political left will have a program to rescue the
country. They will demand that the wealthy and the big
corporations pay their "fair share," that the unemployed be
put on the public payroll, that new measures be enacted to
protect the poor from an inflation caused by previous federal
measures. Appalled at the size of the deficits they have voted,
they will demand that the "bloated defense budget" be pared
down again, in favor of spending for "human resources." And
government will be called upon to step in and save the situation government itself created.

If the political contest of 1976 issues in a verdict for the
liberal point of view, then the time may well have come to
call the rectory for the monsignor to come perform the last
rites over the enterprise system.

Nor will that be the only consequence. For ten years, as
the United States has rested or pulled gently on its oars, the
Soviet Union has made unprecedented advances in conventional and strategic weapons. The day cannot be distant when
the Central Committee decides the hour has come to begin
translating its military gains into diplomatic and political advantage. To cut further into defense now is to trifle with
more than the armaments industry.

For the nation's sake the right must join the debate. By
1976, Americans will have had their fill of Keynesianism and
the "new economics," of deficits spending and "full employment budgets." Indeed, life in America in the late forties and
fifties, when the consumer price index was rising an average
of just above 2 percent a year, and unemployment averaged
4.5 percent, evokes nostalgia when placed along side what the
geniuses and planners of the "New Economics" of the sixties
and seventies have produced.

By 1976, the country should be receptive to another message. The central role of the politicians in creating the current economic crisis must not be forgotten. And what the

public sector produced, the private sector, released from the twin burdens of taxation and regulation, can clean up.

There is no way out of the current crunch without sacrifices. But those sacrifices should come at the expense of the "public sector" which has prospered from the inflation, and not the private sector which has borne the brunt of two recessions, and the worst inflation and unemployment in generations. While unemployment was running last winter around 18 percent in the auto capital of the nation, it was running under 2 percent in the federal bureaucracy. This is where the cuts should come. The demand in '76 should be for government to reduce its army of dependents, to back out of the money markets, to begin living within income, to lift its dead hand from the commerce of the country.

Budget cuts and tax relief should be the issues of the right in '76. What the nation requires is a transfer of resources from nonproducers to producers, monetary growth not to exceed productivity, a budget balance that will block government from monopolizing the capital markets, a restructuring of the tax code to encourage savings and investment, rather than consumption—and some politicians willing to tell the people the truth: The days of wine and roses are over.

The "old-time religion" of fiscal and monetary prudence did not fail the country in recent years. For, as Chesterton said of Christianity, it was never really tried.

Indeed, in running itself ever deeper into debt, government has followed the nation's example. The postwar prosperity of this country has been built on an Everest of debt, a mountain that has risen from $400 billion at the end of World War II, to more than $2.5 trillion.

Of that figure, no less than $1 trillion is in corporate debt, $600 billion in mortgage debt, $500 billion in federal debt, $200 billion in state and local government debt, and another $200 billion in consumer debt. As a fall issue of *Business Week*, devoted to "The Debt Economy," observed:

. . . the U.S. economy is leveraged as never before. There is nearly $8 of debt per $1 of money supply, more than double the figure of 10 years ago. Corporate debt amounts to more than 15 times after-tax profits, compared with under 8 times in 1955. Household debts amount to 93% of disposable income, compared with 65% in 1955. U.S. banks have lent billions overseas through Eurocurrency markets that did not exist in 1955.[2]

Like the foolish grasshopper, the country has been on a summer-long frolic, consuming all it gathers—and ahead is the winter.

IV

Budget cutting is not unlike the medical surgery to which it is commonly compared. Everyone considers modern surgery a boon to mankind; few exhibit enthusiasm going under the knife. Thus, President Ford's recommended cuts in popular programs in '74, and his veto commitments in the State of the Union showed a measure of leadership.

Given the composition of the Ninety-fourth Congress, however, it was a foregone conclusion those cuts would never be made. The near unanimity with which the Ninety-fourth rejected the President's modest proposal to require food stamp beneficiaries to pay 30 percent rather than 23 percent of their net income for subsidized food was a harbinger of things to come.

Still, simple justice is on the President's side. For government *has* prospered mightily in the recent inflation. Taxpayers by the millions have been driven into higher brackets, without compensating increases in purchasing power. Artificial inventory profits have been created for corporations, on which real taxes are eventually paid.

While there is not a snowball's chance of enactment, a freeze on all government salaries would be a welcome initial step. Government, at all levels, in the last decade and a half, despite the party in power in Washington, has become the giant featherbed of the Democratic Party. Pay raises in the Washington bureaucracy—except at the top, and except for judges, where they are justified and needed—have more than kept pace with inflation. And the plague of unemployment ravaging the countryside has been kept outside the castle walls of the U.S. Government.

It is no coincidence that the suburban counties surrounding Washington—where government is the first employer—such as Montgomery, Fairfax and Arlington—have per capita incomes at or near the highest in the nation. When Gerald Ford took office, among his first requests of his old colleagues was that still another 5 percent federal pay hike be deferred—postponed for three months. He was over-ruled by both Houses.

Beyond the freeze, an end should be written to the principle of "comparability" in pay between civil servants and the cream of private enterprise. Civil servants have legislated benefits, protections and job security few private firms can match. To give government employees the same or superior pay is to create an enormous magnet drawing people away from the sector of the economy which produces the wealth of the country and into that sector which consumes it. The incentives should be structured to point in the opposite direction.

Freezing government salaries until they were less competitive with private enterprise—setting them finally at, say 75 percent or 80 percent—would require civil servants to exchange economic advantage for job security. The cost of government would diminish. Much of the current attraction the federal payroll has for white collar workers would disappear. Congress, however, far from requiring sacrifices of federal employees, refused even to hold their pay raises to the President's requested 5 percent.

The same principle might beneficially be applied to the highest echelons of government. Congressionally-legislated pay cuts, even if modest, for themselves, the Cabinet, the President and White House staff, would do more to raise the esteem of politicians than all their rhetoric. The morale of the nation in fighting inflation might improve dramatically if

Americans saw their elected leaders in the trenches beside them—sharing the sacrifices.

Other benefits would accrue. If federal pay were lower than private industry, senior bureaucrats might, after a period of service, be tempted by the greener pastures of private enterprise. A more regular turnover would occur within the bureaucracy; high posts would continually open up to new and younger men and women. Hardening of the arteries, that common ailment of all bureaucracies, might better be prevented. Further, men in Congress and in the supergrades might more readily risk their careers, on matters of principle, if standing by principle did not risk as well their standing in the top 2 percent of Americans in annual income.

Public office was once a public trust entailing personal sacrifice. Today, however, it is among the most rewarding of trades. Cutting the pay of the highest federal officials would mean more elected and chosen public officials who would have spent years outside government earning their way in a society which must bear the brunt of today's financially and politically lucrative liberal idealism.

Late in July 1975, before departing on its fifth vacation of the session, the Ninety-fourth Congress reflected briefly on these arguments. Then, within 24 hours, both Houses voted to award their membership and all senior bureaucrats, this year and every year hence, an automatic cost-of-living salary increase, to spare themselves and future bureaucrats and office-holders from the economic consequences of the inflation they have jointly inflicted upon the country. On returning from Helsinki, President Ford signed the measure into law.

V

The President's State of the Union commitment to veto new social programs should bring at least temporary postponement of national health insurance. If so, the nation will not be without benefit from the current economic conditions.

Nor will the Republican Party, which advanced this scheme so contradictory to its principles. Despite the propaganda, ours and theirs, there is no national "health care crisis" in America justifying use of such a term or the transfer of such resources.

In the early fifties, about half the American people were covered by health insurance; today five-in-six. Federal expenditures for health have already ballooned from $2 billion a decade ago to $28 billion, in fiscal 1976, $20 billion of which is earmarked for the poor. The nation has built more hospital rooms than it can fill. Infant mortality rates which were 78 per 1,000 for blacks, and 43 per 1,000 for whites in 1940 have plunged respectively to 28 and 16. If there was ever a "health care crisis" in the U.S.A., it came and went, unnoticed, long ago.

The economic conditions of 1975 afford the Republican Party, as well, with legitimate grounds for abandoning upon the doorstep of Congress, the "welfare reform" HEW is busily crafting from the dog-eared blueprints of the Family Assistance Plan.

Consider how the scheme most often mentioned—a guaranteed annual income of $3,500 for every household—the subsidy being reduced by 50 cents for every dollar earned—would work.

Take the manual laborer working now for $2 an hour, a forty-hour week, at $4,160 per annum.

Under Big FAP, as *Human Events* has chistened the program, the worker would have his subsidy reduced by one-half of his earned income, i.e. the $3,500 would be reduced by $2,080, one-half of $4,160. This would leave his total income at a combination of the $4,160 earned, plus the $1,420 in federal subsidies, i.e., a total of $5,580, which appears at first glance a significant improvement over what he is earning today.

Proponents tell us that the "working poor" would take to the plan like a duck to water, that those on welfare would be captivated by the work ethic, and the welfare problem would at last be solved.

Closer inspection, however, shows that our laborer would be presented with a set of choices pointing him in the same direction millions have already taken—permanent life on the dole.

A) He can retire at once, and loaf the rest of his life on the $3,500 a year subsidy, which is 83 percent of current income. B) Or he can continue digging ditches day-in and day-out and increase his family income by $2,080 a year to $5,580.

Who today will dig ditches for $2,080 a year—or $1 an hour? How many Americans would not retire, at a moment's notice, if they could do so at 83 percent of current income?

How long does it take to absorb the wisdom of Franklin Roosevelt's warning in the State of the Union, forty years ago?

> The lessons of history . . . show conclusively . . . that continued dependence upon relief induces a spiritual and moral dis-integration fundamentally destructive to the national fibre. To dole out relief is to administer a narcotic, a subtle destroyer of the human spirit . . . the Federal Government must and shall quit this business of relief.[3]

Consider what the sensitive social conscience of men in power has wrought.

By making welfare in some cases as generous as the national minimum wage, politicians have encouraged the lazier among the poor to abandon work altogether and live off the taxes of the middle class. By taking over the traditional role of the husband, that of family provider, government has given millions of poor women the economic security they need to throw the father out of the house. Indeed, were welfare payments suddenly raised to $20,000 a year, a goodly percentage of middle-class married women might do the same.

The welfare problem in the United States is a social disaster of our own creation. It will endure until the life-style of those in "menial dead-end jobs" is visibly superior to the living conditions of those with no job at all. And it will only grow if the "constituency of conscience" in both parties gets its way. Necessity makes men work. And while it might appear mean-spirited to say so, remove that necessity and many men are no more interested in a hard day's work for a day's pay than are many of the children of the very rich.

Those champions of the poor and oppressed who sleep better at night in Kenwood and McLean for having hiked the minimum wage, for having raised the welfare floor, are as much the friend of the poor and the black as the soft-hearted bartender is of the alcoholic.

As Dr. Roger Freeman, the economist and former White House assistant, whose testimony more than any other prevented enactment of H. R. 1, has written:

> It is interesting to contemplate how clean the subways, streets and parks are in Moscow and Leningrad—with whole swarms of men and women cleaning them all the time. But then, the Soviet Union offers no welfare or unemployment pay to able-bodied persons and its minimum wage was lifted from $44 to $66 a month only last January. Ours is $277. Minimum pay was just raised in New York, and a parallel move is now being demanded on the federal level, which would force large additional numbers on welfare. The Soviet Union has a rule (Article 12 of its Constitution) that "he who does not work, neither shall he eat." In the United States that principle of St. Paul has long yielded to the welfare state precept that the ties between work and income should be weakened and eventually cut.[4]

Since Dr. Freeman wrote those lines in 1970, the minimum wage has been elevated at the federal level to $398 a month by 1977; and welfare rolls have very nearly doubled again.

VI

To understand why the budget is out of control, one must understand the process through which its inexorable growth is achieved. A typical scenario runs thus: Liberal politicians and like-minded fellows in the press announce one morning that they have stumbled upon a heretofore unnoticed "crisis" within society. It may be the "crisis of the cities," the "crisis of hunger" or the "crisis of poverty." The networks then focus their cameras upon some particularly graphic aspect, proving the "crisis" does indeed exist. Having pricked the nation's social conscience, the press and politicians then loudly charge the incumbent administration with indifference and insensitivity. Government responds with a dramatic increase in federal assistance, which contribution will then categorically be dismissed as "hopelessly inadequate."

Consider hunger. Early in the Nixon years, Senator George McGovern and CBS News jointly discovered "Hunger in America." Even though the Nixon administration was already spending considerably more than its Democratic predecessors for food assistance, the regime was charged with indifference and insensitivity to the widespread malnutrition eating at the vitals of society. In some especially appealing and fraudulent footage, CBS showed the nation film of a premature baby near death, and informed the country this was an American child dying of starvation. The public reaction was immediate, and the President acted. The food stamp program which was feeding around 3 million at a cost of some $270 million in 1969 was by late 1974 feeding more than 16 million at an annual cost approaching $4 billion. In Dane County, Wisconsin, *The New York Times* found that two-thirds of the food stamps were going to that historically underprivileged and oppressed class, college students.

Seeing a food assistance program for the truly needy ballooning into another general welfare program, President Ford sought to cut it back toward its original purpose, reducing the number of eligibles, and requiring beneficiaries to pay a larger share of the cost of their own food. Both he and his Administration—the most generous in history with food assistance—were savaged in Congress and the press for an act of particularly Republican cruelty. CBS sent its reporter into Arkansas to find two or three women who would indicate to the nation how terribly their family would suffer. Collaterally, a New York-based "public interest law firm" demanded that the Federal Government conduct a nationwide search for some 20 million additional Americans it believed were eligible, but who had not yet signed up for subsidized food.

From a modest program to feed the destitute, food stamps degenerated into a vast scheme for transferring to working- and middle-class families the food bills of the welfare class.

And while the working and middle class pay, the public sector and its clients benefit.

The networks, of course, and the metropolitan press win awards, audience ratings and plaudits for their dramatization of crises. The government gains a net increase in the share of the nation's wealth it controls. And the liberal politician, having flexed his moral muscles and paraded his "concern," has purchased another bloc of voters with Treasury—or taxpayers'—dollars. Jeffrey Hart is a longtime observer of the process.

For a certain kind of person, problems are much more interesting than solutions. And the reason is that the McGoverns and all the other hunger warriors are not primarily concerned about hunger, really, and not about something so pedestrian as food. Rather, they desire to dramatize their capacity for concern itself. It is the dramatization that is all important. Therefore the hunger politician of 1969 can suddenly become the pollution politician of 1970. The whole idea is to set up the correct vibrations with a particular constituency.

When you have watched this process go on for some time, you discern that it even has a quasi-religious dimension. Dramatizing concern, setting up the correct vibrations, establishes a politician as a Man of Goodwill, one of the saved, a member of the moral elect.[5]

The late and unlamented presidential commission of Governor Otto Kerner and Mayor John Lindsay, which bore the name of the former, warned seven years ago that we were becoming "two societies." But it is not "white racism" as the commission alleged, but government, itself, through its social policies, that has brought this about. America *is* two societies. One is an expanding army of millions, utterly dependent upon government for education, medical care, food and shelter. The other is a society of producers and laborers, blue collar and white collar, increasingly bitter about carrying that government and army upon their backs.

VII

In his book, *The Real America*, documenting the material progress of society over the past four decades, Mr. Ben Wattenberg wonders aloud why liberals and civil rights leaders rarely acknowledge the steady improvements in American life.

The reasons are not distant. If politicians should tell Americans the truth, that ours is a good and great country, that our society has been extraordinarily prosperous, that the wealth is widely distributed, that, excepting crime, our social problems are as nothing compared to what they were decades ago, who would support further expansion in the size and power of government?

Portraying America as the heart of darkness enables the politician to cast himself as a missionary of light and justice, who must be granted sweeping authority to set things right. Liberals are not interested in past progress; they are interested in future power.

To gain that power, they must convince the nation that the current situation is intolerable. Thus, John Gardner insists that the "nation disintegrates," while Senator Muskie wails, "we have reached the point where men would rather die than live another day in America." Senator Mondale declares, "The sickening truth is that this country is rapidly coming to resemble South Africa," and Gary Hart observes that ours is a "society teetering somewhere near the brink of moral bankruptcy and collapse."[6]

Yet, consider but a few of those matters about which we have heard regularly the doomsday rhetoric. Is there, for example, truly a "housing crisis" within our cities, a social disorder justifying emergency federal intervention?

According to *Social Indicators, 1973,* a publication of the Office of Management and Budget, only 7 percent of the nation's housing was substandard in 1970 and much of that was in rural America—compared to nearly 50 percent before World War II. Progress in housing has been enormous, and is continuing. Where three-fourths of all black Americans lived in "substandard dwellings" before the war, about one-fourth did in 1970. Again, if America did have a "housing crisis" we were unaware of it at the time, and it has long since passed away.

What of the "population crisis," the terrible crowding and congestion of our cities? Are we destined to end our days like the experimental rats who overpopulated their closed environment and destroyed themselves? Again, hardly. The population of many of our oldest cities is actually declining. It is new cities like Dallas and Phoenix and Los Angeles and the suburbs that have shown the enormous growth in the postwar era. And they are anything but examples of "crowded living conditions." Further, the growth in population today is running at the lowest level in decades. Between 1900 and 1975, we very nearly tripled our population of 75 million. Why should Americans be paralyzed with concern that we shall add by the end of the century roughly half the number of people we have added to our population since 1940?

In the Netherlands, population density is 829 per square mile; in England, 593, in India, 426—in the United States, 57. Even the most densely populated of our states like Rhode Island and Connecticut are pleasant places to live. Americans have no population crisis. They have no population problem, other than the likelihood that forty years from now, the proportion of those in retirement and on pensions will be far greater in relation to the work force than it is today.

What about the "dropouts"—that soaring social problem of which we heard so much a half decade ago? Statistics show that in 1940, only 48 percent of white adults, aged twenty to twenty-four, had finished high school; only 15 percent of the blacks. Today, the respective figures are 85 percent and 70 percent. If dropouts are a social problem, the problem belonged to the generation getting ready for retirement.

As for higher education, where there were 1.5 million in colleges in the U.S. thirty-five years ago, there are 10 million today. And the percentage of blacks on campus exceeds that of some white ethnic groups. There is simply no problem of access today to public education or higher education, worth characterizing as a serious social concern.

And how goes the "war on poverty?"

Well as usual for the poverty warriors. As for the poor themselves, they continue, as they have throughout the history of this country, to move into the ranks of the working class. In the last decade 15 million Americans crossed the poverty line, and the percentage of those categorized as "poor" was cut in half. This figure does not even take into account the cash value of the sweeping array of social services and benefits provided the lower income, from food stamps to scholarships, housing subsidies to health care. The gap between black and white also continues to close. In 1947, blacks earned half as much as whites; today it is almost two-thirds. And were only blacks under thirty-five taken into account, the gap has almost disappeared.

Even when poor and elderly blacks are factored into the equation, black America is approaching roughly the same level of income as was attained by the entire nation in 1957 and 1958—when Professor John Kenneth Galbraith proclaimed ours to be The Affluent Society.

As mentioned, there is no true health care crisis in America. Americans live longer. Old diseases have given way to new cures. Infant mortality rates have fallen dramatically since before the war. Expenditures on health care are truly enormous at federal, state, local and personal levels.

As for pollution, the situation in most cities is better than it was two decades ago; appreciably better than a few years ago.

Indeed, the country faces less of a danger from pollution of the air, than from pollution of the airwaves with the semi-hysterical ravings of individuals who, in earlier times, would have been denied a license to carry a sandwich board in Times Square announcing the end of the world.

VIII

When one considers the genuine perils confronted by the men and women who settled this land, when one recalls the social injustices of a century past, it becomes evident that the danger to democracy is less in the objective conditions of society than in the quality of America's leadership class. They are infecting a whole country with their chronic pessimism.

And the motivation of these men and their political allies seems less and less disinterested. Take, for example, the situation in transportation.

With the rise in oil and gasoline prices, politicians have begun to wage war on the private automobile, demanding its replacement with rapid transit systems, built and operated by Government.

But do Americans prefer rapid transit, and would they use it? For decades they have been abandoning the mass transit system for the automobile. Between 1960 and 1970 those Americans traveling to work by car rose from 82 percent to 87 percent—a rather convincing vote for automobile travel. In New York City, subway ridership has plunged to the lowest level since 1918, when the city had 2.5 million fewer residents. The city has lost a million daily riders in a decade.

Why does not government build upon this bias, in favor of cars and highways, in solving the energy crisis? Europeans pay three times the price Americans do for gasoline. Surely, by letting the price of gasoline rise, forcing car pools to form, by extending anti-pollution regulations, by tripling the number of taxi medallions, by allowing the return of jitneys, by increasing the number of busses and allowing private companies to compete in providing mass transit, the government could use the market forces and the existing splendid highway system to solve any transportation problem that might arise.

But that would never do. Because it leaves the role of government too small. The men of government want rapid mass transit in America's cities, and the number of autos reduced, because that would mean government, rather than individuals, would dictate how people travel in America. This is a question of who decides; it is a question of who spends the resources of society: individuals on their cars, or the government on its trains.

In the nation's capital, the government is building a subway system, the cost overruns on which would be a national scandal were the money being spent for Air Force cargo planes instead of a 98-mile hole in the ground. What was to be accomplished for $2.5 billion in taxes will cost, at the least, $4.5 billion—and one is pressed to find a politician who thinks we will get off that lightly. Until the Washington system and the San Francisco system are in place and running profitably, Americans ought to oppose new billions for rapid transit. The economy needs tax relief more than a new transportation system.

IX

The point is not to deny social problems exist in the post-industrial society. The rising crime rate menaces the freedom and security of every American, even as the energy shortage threatens our independence of action in foreign policy, and the economic security of the West. But this chapter does suggest that many of those situations defined as "crises" are not crises at all. They are being fabricated, manufactured, by politicians and the press to bring about a fundamental restructuring of society. They are being used as the convenient pegs upon which the political left is hanging its demands that a larger share of the nation's wealth and authority be taken away from the private sector, which pays them no mind, and transferred to the public sector, where their voice is supreme. Their crisis-mongering may be about the horrors of pollution and poverty and unsafe products and price-gouging and profiteering; their thoughts are upon power. For themselves.

When Gerald R. Ford warned the liberal Democrats of the Ninety-fourth Congress that if we did not mend our ways, half the nation's national product in fifteen years would pass through the hands of government, he was threatening B'rer Rabbit with the briar patch.

Republicans have to pick up their chips and get out of this game. You cannot play table stakes with Muskie, McGovern, Kennedy and Humphrey. We cannot match what the Democratic Party can offer its favored interest groups and voting blocs in the way of federal funds—because most Republicans have in the back of their minds the old-fashioned notion that the money they are spending is not theirs to give.

For the Republican Party to accept the Democrat-media definition of the social problems facing the United States, and to compete in how generous we can be with public funds to "solve these problems," is to lose before we suit up and take the field. If there is any opportunity for the Republican Party, it is to reject, to ignore altogether, the Democrat-media list of priorities and to submit to the electorate an agenda of our own.

Let them debate, by themselves and with each other, the horrors the Central Intelligence Agency allegedly perpetuated against Jane Fonda, the necessity to give government bureaucrats the right to strike, and the historic injustices that explain the hooliganism of the Menominee warriors. And let us emulate the Governor of Alabama in the spring of '72, when he tore up the media's recommended list of debate topics and forced onto the national agenda *his* issues—bussing, high taxes, crime and the arrogance of the bureaucracy. Though Wallace simply ignored the liberal issues, he prevailed in the liberals' party. There was a kernel of truth in that sticker pasted on the rear bumper of many of the pick-up trucks and station wagons in the South. "It takes courage. Wallace has it. Do you?"

Folks who run around saying, "Custer had it coming," are not with us anyway. Our constituency cheers the Seventh Cavalry.

Unlike the Democrats, whose success depends upon portraying government as the engine of progress, Republicans should portray government for what it has become, a vast machine for the redistribution of wealth and resources away from individuals and institutions, which produce it, over to the bureaucracy, the politicians and their preferred clients.

Reflect. Is it not the liberals' artistic and academic friends who get the grants from the federal endowments for arts and the humanities? Is it not journalists of their persuasion who are given the large salaries and big fees for pontificating on "public" television? Is it not their children hired by Vista and the Peace Corps, and selected for the Reggie Heber Smith fellowships to work out their ideology in Legal Services? Is it not their Naderite collaborators who will wind up with the positions of authority in a new federal consumer protection agency? Has it not been the professional bureaucrats, planners, consultants and professors whose power, prestige and income have grown directly proportional to the growth in federal power the last decade and a half?

For the political left, Washington has become the New Golconda. Government of, by and for the liberals is their benefactor, and the nation's burden.

☆

Beyond Detente

I

Not since the autumn of 1940 have the prospects of the democracies and the West appeared so grim.

In the spring of 1975, three nations and almost 30 million people in South Vietnam, Cambodia and Laos were swept into the Communist camp. They are the first nations since Cuba a decade and a half ago incorporated into the Communist world. And with the United States still war-weary and disunited, unwilling to make another stand in Southeast Asia, there appears nothing to prevent the tide of Asian Communism from rolling down the balance of Southeast Asia until it reaches the Straits of Malacca. When that day comes, there will likely be nothing left of Asian confidence in the credibility and capacity of the United States as an ally.

Already, in the Western Pacific, the first of many questions are being raised, from Australia to Japan, about the reliability of the United States. The foreign policy of the Philippines has undergone reassessment; the vital American bases in the islands are no longer guaranteed. Taiwan, ostracized by the U.N., watches apprehensively as Peking makes more insistent its demand that the United States abide by the understandings inherent in the Shanghai communique.

The Korean peninsula is closer to war than it has been in more than twenty years. The North Korean Communists, having watched their comrades in Hanoi outlast and finally defeat American policy, are anxious to seize the moment, emulate the example, drive the Americans off the mainland of Northeast Asia, and unite all Korea under Communist rule.

If a North Korean invasion comes, it will direct itself toward the Southern capital of Seoul, only several dozen miles from the DMZ. On the direct avenue of approach to the South Korean capital, there stands today an American army division. Should that invasion come, then, the United States— whose people wish desperately to avoid another land war in Asia—would be faced with the choice of either committing massive air and sea power against North Korea, turning tail and running, or watching their own soldiers and South Korean allies overrun and defeated by a Communist army.

On the Asian sub-continent, Bangladesh appears a terminal case. India, formerly the world's largest democracy, recipient of billions in United States food and economic assistance, is almost a Soviet ally, as anti-American as any regime in Asia.

In the Persian Gulf, the sheiks, shahs and kings, heady with the power that comes as a consequence of being situated atop the world's largest known reserves of petroleum, are readying another price hike for the West. Aware of the central importance of the region to the democracies, the Soviet Navy is as visible in those waters as was the British fleet decades ago. Meanwhile, the vital investment capital of the West pours by the billions, in dollars and pounds sterling, into the coffers of the Middle East.

Between Israel and her neighbors, there is, in MacArthur's phrase, an "entirely new war."

With the Arabs controlling the oil upon which Western Europe and the Third World depend for survival, Israel is as isolated diplomatically as Rhodesia. Reflecting that isolation was the roaring reception accorded the guerrilla Yasser Arafat at the United Nations, in 1974, which convinced even the infinitely tolerant *Washington Post* to write off the General Assembly as a "political and moral slag heap."[1] Dominant in manpower, partially rearmed by the Soviets, possessed of adequate resources for the long struggle, the Arabs now look forward with confidence to victory in the final Arab-Israeli war, if not the next collision of arms.

The Israelis, an island of a few million in a hostile sea of tens of millions, pressed financially as no other democracy, almost devoid of sympathizers outside the United States, dependent upon a military lifeline extending halfway around the earth, are beginning to understand there are some things which courage, ingenuity and arms cannot accomplish. The God of the twentieth century remains on the side of the big battalions.

The shifting military balance on land is reflected in the Mediterranean. The great inland sea is no longer the *mare nostrum* of the West. A Soviet Mediterranean squadron is present whose surface vessels regularly outnumber the Sixth Fleet. Unlike 1958, when President Eisenhower sent the Marines ashore in Lebanon, to ineffectual bluster from Moscow, in 1973 it was Mr. Brezhnev who credibly threatened military intervention with his airborne divisions, and it was Washington issuing the warnings.

The Cyprus situation remains tense and unresolved.

Relations between Greece and Turkey, our southernmost NATO allies, are poisonous. Anti-Americanism is rampant in Athens. And though the Turks have been among the most reliable of allies, the Ninety-fourth Congress has permanently crippled relations with Ankara, to ingratiate itself with Greek-Americans.

Across the Adriatic, the political drift and continuing economic disorder in Italy present the Communists with the greatest opportunity since 1948 for a share of power. Neither an end to democracy in Italy, nor Rome's departure from NATO, is beyond the realm of possibility.

Europe ends with the Pyrenees, Napoleon once contemptuously commented. Beyond those mountains today, the stability of despotism gives way to uncertainty. The authoritarian Portuguese regime which permitted use of the Azores to the United States for its emergency airlift to Israel in 1973 has fallen. An Armed Forces Movement, saturated with and sympathetic to the Communists in Lisbon, is in power. The Azores will not be available in the next Mideast War. The possibility of Portuguese withdrawal from NATO, and Soviet bases on the Atlantic, cannot be ruled out.

In Spain, General Franco, Europe's most implacable anti-Communist and since the thirties special *bête noire* of Western liberals, nears the end. His passing will leave a vacuum in Madrid which left, as well as right, is preparing to fill. Before his death, Lenin is said to have observed that the next soviet state would be on the Iberian peninsula. His prediction appears more realistic today. Among the littoral states of the Mediterranean Sea, there is not a single country where the American naval presence is as welcome as it was two decades ago.

Every economy in Western Europe has been injured, some crippled, by the worst peacetime disorder since the Depression. Every industrial nation remains a potential blackmail victim of the Arab oil cartel. In the judgment of some diplomats, European behavior in the Middle East war of 1973 justified the descriptions craven and cowardly. If they would buckle under to Abu Dhabi and Kuwait, asked one analyst, how well would they stand up to the Red Army?

Writing from Paris last fall, the *New York Times* columnist C. L. Sulzberger perceived the "Signposts to Disaster."

France, traditionally Europe's most prosperous land has more unemployment than any time since World War II and work stoppages ripple across the country. England's flat broke, floundering economically and caught in an endless Irish conflict, last battle of the seventeenth-century religious wars.

Italy is mired in chaos. Portugal hovers on the edge of tumult and Spain may soon approach a similar border when Generalissimo Franco dies. Japan's dynamism shows signs of dissolving like a wet noodle; South Asia

is disintegrating; much of Africa starves, and the richest
of the oil sheiks have accumulated so much money they
don't know even how to budget it.[2]

In Central Europe, where NATO faces the Warsaw Pact,
the military balance has never been more favorable to the
East since the onset of the Cold War. Western grumbling
over the burden of arms budgets grows louder, while the
Soviets conclude one of the truly great military buildups in
history. Undisputedly the world's leading conventional power
on land, sea and air, the Soviets have now achieved strategic
parity with the United States and are reaching for strategic
and naval superiority.

Four years ago, in *Foreign Policy* magazine, Andrew J.
Pierre wrote:

> The role of momentum should not be overlooked.
> There is a wide psychological canyon between a nation
> that is catching up and achieving parity in the conven-
> tional as well as nuclear arms, and another nation that has
> or is losing its superiority . . .
>
> There is a real danger that the Soviet leaders will now
> see opportunities for political exploitation around the
> globe that were not available before, and that they will
> be tempted to take greater risks. The mere availability
> of a new global military capability can generate pressures
> for its use.[3]

Facing the Soviet and Prussian divisions in East Germany,
if the West's media can be believed, are American and allied
divisions, afflicted with drugs and racism and convulsed over
such questions as beer in the barracks, union rights for enlisted men, and the wearing of hair to shoulder length. One
wonders if Marshal Grechko confronts demands for hair nets
from within the Red Army; or if Admiral Gorshkov maintains a quota of Uzbeks in the Baltic Fleet.

Even as U.S. diplomats attempt to negotiate mutual pull-
backs from Central Europe, American politicians demand uni-

lateral withdrawals. Why should 210 million Americans be responsible for the defense of 300 million Europeans against 250 million Russians? So the question runs.

Meanwhile, in the United States, the networks and news organizations seek out and publicize stories on discrimination and discord in the ranks. The Congress looks to the defense budget for the dollars to subsidize the social spending that will save the marginal seats in '76. And the military-industrial complex that inspires the greatest anxiety and antagonism among writers, intellectuals and politicians is centered not in Moscow but in Arlington, Virginia.

Nearly twenty-five years ago, a less affluent America, facing a Soviet challenge not half so grave or all-extensive as that posed today, was investing, without whimpering, twice the percentage of its federal budget, twice the percentage of GNP, in defense. Today, even our reduced burden is proclaimed almost universally to be too onerous to bear.

Not for a third of a century has the West seemed so near to the end of its tether. And the question is why.

II

The NATO countries are not inferior to the Warsaw Pact, either in wealth or in numbers. With the United States and Canada added to the balance, they are vastly superior. In the West, the rates of productivity growth are higher, the pools of skilled manpower larger, the educational levels superior, the economic systems more productive and flexible. The Soviet Union, most advanced of the Communist countries, must import not only technology from the West, but food.

Yet, as in the thirties, the leaders of the Western democracies seem incapable of asking of their own people sacrifices, for security, commensurate with what the Communist regimes easily impose. In addition to keeping at the ready superior manpower and conventional armaments in Central Europe, the Soviets maintain a million-man army along the Chinese frontier and dozens of active divisions in reserve. As a measure of the lack of vision and spirit of sacrifice in the West, perhaps the most prominent political figure on the Eurasian land mass arguing insistently and regularly for keeping a vigorous NATO alliance tied to the United States is Chou En-lai of the Peoples Republic of China.

The shifting balance of power, away from the advanced and affluent West, to the economically retarded and backward East, could not have come about without the acquiescence of the former.

Consistently, in the last decade, Soviet capabilities were underestimated and Soviet intentions misjudged, by political leaders, including those in the United States. If a pivot point can be fixed in history, it was the aftermath of the Cuban missile crisis.

Backed by the enormous strategic superiority over the Soviets that was Eisenhower's legacy to the Democratic Administration, enjoying naval supremacy in the Caribbean Sea, President Kennedy, his invasion force building, forced the Soviets to dismantle before the world their missile installations and withdraw their rockets from Cuba.

The two nations took away separate lessons from the first nuclear confrontation. The American leaders said to themselves: never again must the great powers approach so close to the brink of war. The Soviets: never again will it be the East that backs away from confrontation with the United States.

Driven by the memory of October '62, the Soviets over the last dozen years undertook one of the most remarkable military buildups in history. Traditional Soviet superiority in ground forces, tanks, artillery, tactical aircraft and air defense have become overwhelming. Traditional Russian inferiority on the high seas has become a thing of the past as the Soviets have launched a blue-water navy that sails on every ocean of the world. Most significant, the Soviet inferiority in strategic weapons at the time of Cuba has been transformed into something approaching marginal superiority over the United States.

If they act thus in the green wood, said Winston Churchill

early in the Cold War, how will they act in the dry? We are entering the dry wood now.

Looking back upon that Cuban missile crisis, which appeared such an American triumph, Richard Whalen has penned a more realistic interpretation:

> This, then, was the concrete outcome of the missile crisis: an American agreement permanently to tolerate what had earlier been branded intolerable—a base for Soviet military power and Communist subversion within the Western hemisphere.
>
> Thus, while we respected the Soviet sphere, the Soviets were no longer bound to respect ours. While we took as the objective of our military strength, the maintenance of stability, the Soviets took as theirs the overthrow of the status quo. While we identified nuclear war as the greatest danger, the Soviets identified nuclear inferiority as the greatest obstacle to their freedom of action.[4]

So long as the Soviets were willing to make the sacrifices, the United States could do nothing to prevent their becoming a nuclear superpower of the first order. What was not inevitable, however, was Soviet parity, or the alarming margins of superiority the Soviets have attained in the numbers and capacity of their missiles. With an economic base twice that of the USSR, the United States needed only half the relative effort to maintain superiority.

That we did not make the sacrifice in weapons research, development and deployment was the result of a conscious decision by U.S. leaders like Robert McNamara who looked on benignly as the Soviets closed the gap, believing that in parity lies peace.

The Johnson-McNamara decision to relax upon the oars, as the Soviets pulled abreast, was ratified by President Nixon and his national security adviser. Faced with a Congress which by only a single vote approved a partial missile defense, the President and Dr. Kissinger decided to make a virtue of necessity. Absolute security for one nation, preached the President's security adviser, means absolute insecurity for all the others. The President echoed the theme: ". . . the only time in the history of the world that we have had any extended periods of peace is when there has been a balance of power." Thus might the statesmen of Carthage have rationalized the rising military and naval power of Rome.

For ten years now, it is difficult to recall *once* when an American President asked for evening television time to alert the nation to the realities of the shifting balance of power. If today Americans remain convinced the United States is as unrivaled on land, sea and air as in 1945 or even 1962, the media alone is not at fault.

III

In the early seventies, in Western intellectual circles, it was fashionable to disparage the Soviet Union as a "nation of hardhats," its leadership as "third-rate bureaucrats," while fawning upon the aging first-generation revolutionary purists who have made of China the only great nation on earth where the arch-terrorist, Joseph Stalin, remains officially revered.

But when one considers the relative achievements, of both powers, the records of the three men to have served since the death of Lenin, as First Secretary of the Communist Party, are not unimpressive.

Under Stalin, the Communist Party consolidated control over the far-flung reaches of the Romanovs' empire. A hundred million Eastern Europeans were brought under the hegemony of Moscow. The world's most populous state, China, passed from West to East; and the USSR became the world's second nuclear power.

Under Khrushchev, the Eastern European empire was consolidated and sealed. The Soviet Union led the world into the space age. A Communist outpost was established in the Western Hemisphere, on the doorstep of the United States; and an American President unofficially rescinded the Monroe

Doctrine, cornerstone of American foreign policy for four-teen decades.

Under Brezhnev, the Soviet Union has become a super-power to rival any in the history of man. Its armies dominate Central Europe; its navies sail every ocean of the globe; its strategic power, in signed agreement with the United States, will never again become inferior to any country. The ancient Russian imperialist ambitions toward the Middle East and the Persian Gulf are closer to realization than at any period in history. And the West has formally recognized the Soviet sphere in Eastern Europe, and the Soviet colony of East Germany. Not Peter the Great, not Catherine II managed such conquests.

The post-war Russian rise to empire has not been uninter-rupted. There have been counter-revolutions in Chile, and an earlier, bloodier one in Indonesia, fifth most populous nation on earth, which decimated the party. There have been defeats for Soviet arms in the Middle East, and the humiliat-ing withdrawal from Cuba. There have been revolutions in almost every satellite state in Eastern Europe. Under the Nixon-Kissinger diplomacy, the Soviet influence in Egypt and the Middle East was diminished in the wake of the Yom Kippur War. And China's departure from the Soviet orbit was no less a blow to the Soviet Union than the loss of Henry VIII's England and Protestant Europe to Catholic Rome in the Reformation. But, looking back, it can be said that the twentieth century has not brought an end to empires, only to the empires of the West. Thirty years ago Communism ruled the Soviet Union, the Baltic states and Mongolia, 7 percent of the world's population, 18 percent of the earth's surface. Today, 1.4 billion people, 35 percent of the world's popula-tion, and more than a quarter of the world's land area are governed by Communist regimes in 17 nations.

And what has been the price of empire?

While America has spent hundreds of billions of dollars in two peninsular wars in Asia, and lost a hundred thousand dead and half a million wounded—as well as her national unity and sense of purpose—the only Soviet combat troops to have fallen in battle since the fall of Berlin died in Eastern Europe stamping out the last sparks of rebellion within the empire. Looking out at the West and the world from behind the Kremlin walls, it would be difficult not to view the future with confidence in the ultimate verdict of history.

IV

What is the nature of the system and society, with which the United States, by history's arrangement and timetable, is locked in ideological struggle? Even to one who has traveled only weeks within the Soviet Union, the truth of C. L. Sulzberger's observation emerges: "The U.S.S.R. is a massive, strange country; a superpower with its head in outer space, with its feet in the mud of poverty, with mighty muscles and fear in its heart."[5]

To travel by rail from Moscow to Leningrad to Kiev and back again is to travel to Russia's great cities of the twentieth century, through towns and villages where the people have not yet left the nineteenth.

Where, for Americans, reality is the present, for the Soviets, as for the Chinese, reality is the future. If there is a single guideline which dictates the allocation of its vast resources, it is to sacrifice the comforts and pleasures of today for the rewards and glories of tomorrow.

Youth, education, science, the Party, the military—these are the pampered sectors of Soviet society. Invariably it is to the schools, the academic institutes, the science centers that the Soviets take their visitors to see the best the system builds. American students may indulge the fantasy of themselves as members of an "oppressed class." To the Soviets, higher education is a privilege, an honor, a passport to the better life, second in value only to membership in the Party.

Outside the Young Pioneer Palace in Kiev, old men and women sweep the streets and clamber atop street cars to hook up the trolleys, while inside the children of Kiev enjoy a cultural and educational facility to rival anything in the United States. Six hours a week they spend there being indoctrinated through films, lectures, classes, magazines and books in the history and glory of Communism and the Soviet Union. At an age when American children are entering first grade, the most promising of the children of Kiev are pledging their allegiance to Communism and faith in Lenin, as "Young Octobrists," even as Catholic school children, on making their first communion, pledge their faith in Jesus Christ. "Give us the child for eight years," said Lenin, "and it will be a Bolshevik forever."[6]

Among the sharpest contrasts one encounters between the societies is the regard in which the relative military establishments are held. In the United States, to ridicule Pentagon demands for "fancy new weapon systems," to be publicly contemptuous of the "military mind," is to mark one as fashionable, *au courant* with modern thinking. Few more damning commentaries can be made upon a public figure than that he exhibits a "Cold War mentality." In the inaugural parades of U.S. Presidents, the military, with the exception of the service academies, seems almost an embarrassing presence. Here, the public display of military vehicles and weaponry is taken to be bad form; not so in Soviet Russia.

In the anniversary celebration of the Bolshevik overthrow of Russian democracy, as troops, armed vehicles, tanks, and missiles of every variety pass before the Politburo above Lenin's Tomb in Red Square, there is no cluck-clucking in the reviewing stand, no great sucking of air as one might anticipate were such a display of military might to come up Pennsylvania Avenue and pass before the President. Rather, on the anniversary of the Great October Revolution, there is enthusiastic applause from the citizens of Moscow, visible pride as the military power of Mother Russia rolls by.

Atop Soviet society, like the visible tip of an iceberg, sits the Party, an elite of some 14,500,000 closed to most Soviet citizens, which determines who shall hold every position of significance within the system, from factory manager to foreign minister. The Party controls all the access roads to prestige, comfort, privilege and power. Seeking out the most industrious and able, judging applicants on merit, intelligence, ability and drive, the Party imposes one indispensable criterion for advancement, Stakhanovite loyalty to the party and dogmatic subservience to the party line.

Even on the extremes of American politics, one has difficulty finding an example of the ideological rigidity one commonly encounters arguing with party members or Komsomol.

Despite detente, there are attitudes common to the new Soviet man that do not bode well for the future. There is a cockiness and confidence about them, a boisterous faith in the superiority of their system, the future of their society, and, if you will, the manifest destiny of the Soviet Union. One cannot discourse for several hours without coming away with the impression that these are individuals who believe the future by right belongs to them, even as the past belongs to the decadent and dying West. One does not catch about them a whiff of that sense of remorse and guilt of which so many Western intellectuals, politicians and journalists fairly reek.

Any failure or shortcoming they trace to the World War. In Tashkent, local youth officials were uninterested in statistics showing Uzbeks behind the Russians in per capita income, and the Russians behind the Germans and Japanese, who suffered similarly in the Great Patriotic War. Rather, they proudly cite statistics of how far they have advanced since the Revolution of 1917; and how well off are Uzbeks in comparison with Afghans and Paks.

Though only 6 percent of the Soviet people are Party members, though Party dogma has little grip on the popular imagination, still, the Party controls the East's destiny; and the Party will present the face of Russia to the West.

But the weaknesses of the Soviet system are as visible as its strengths. The Soviet Union is less a nation, in the sense that Germany and Japan are nations, than it is a great empire of Russians, ruling over nationalities, peoples and states. Non-

Russian minorities comprise half the Soviet population. As a returning correspondent wrote early this year, ". . . the various peoples of the Soviet Union had long been enemies. Centuries of war, conquest and rivalry had turned Georgian against Armenian, Uzbek against Tadzhik, Ukranian against Russian, Russian against Tartar and all against the Jews."[7] In Eastern Europe reside some 100 million Poles, Hungarians, Germans, Bulgarians, Czechs, Slovaks, Rumanians, Albanians and other nationalities, many of them with memories of belonging to independent nations, many of them belonging to races and peoples which bear historic animosity to Mother Russia.

What was said of the Russian Empire in the nineteenth century is even more true of the U.S.S.R. of the twentieth; it is truly the "prison house of nations."

In an age where anti-colonialist and nationalist passions are on the rise from Scotland to Puerto Rico, from Ireland to the Ukraine, the Kremlin cannot loosen its grip for an instant. For the foreseeable future, these minorities present the Soviets with potential internal problems, alongside which the American civil rights revolution will appear trifling. Indeed, alongside the Soviet Union, this "nation of immigrants" is an homogenous society.

Then, too, those hundreds of thousands of soldiers and police assigned to keep the populations inside, and the information, publications and ideas of the dissolute West out, are corroborating witnesses to Communist weakness. Six decades after the Revolution, when most of the adult population in Eastern Europe has been reared on Communism, when almost every Soviet citizen has been educated under the hammer and sickle, still the system cannot attract from millions even the minimum allegiance. No great state in history harbored so many enemies and potential traitors.

Nor could the workers' paradise allow open access to the consumer goods of the West. To do so, given the high cost and shoddy quality of Soviet merchandise, would be to trigger a tidal wave of Western goods flowing into Russia and an outflow of Soviet capital which would dwarf what the West now pays for oil to the Middle East.

V

Confronted with such manifest failures, why cannot the United States look forward with confidence to an ideological struggle between the heirs of the Russian Revolution and the descendants of the American Revolution? It is because Americans are no longer united over the proposition that the struggle should be waged.

The great bipartisan post-war consensus on foreign policy split apart—on the reef of Vietnam. Americans are no longer united about the basic principles of containment that guided U.S. foreign policy under Presidents Truman, Eisenhower, Kennedy, Johnson and Nixon. And, as Walter Lippmann wrote three decades ago, at the height of the World War:

> . . . when a people is divided within itself about the conduct of its foreign relations, it is unable to agree on the determination of its true interest. It is unable to prepare adequately for war or to safeguard successfully its peace. Thus its course in foreign affairs depends, in Hamilton's words not on reflection and choice but on accident and force.[8]

Thus it is today. The political parties, informed opinion, and the nation are divided, deeply, over what American foreign policy should be. There is no consensus over whether troops should be maintained in Europe, no consensus on whether the United States should maintain its commitment to South Korea, no consensus on what stance the United States should take toward the pro-Western authoritarian states of Europe, Asia and Latin America; no consensus even on the question of whether America should maintain military parity with the Soviet Union.

How far we have come. Consider the near unanimity with which the nation supported Eisenhower's dispatch of Marines to Lebanon, and the hysterical reaction among American journalists and intellectuals when, seven years later, President Johnson sent the same Marines, for a similar purpose, to Santo Domingo. Compare the internationalist rhetoric of John F. Kennedy ("We shall pay any price, bear any burden . . .") with the isolationist patter of his youngest brother. Where the Congresses of the mid-sixties gave Lyndon Johnson a blank check to wage war in Vietnam, the current Congress would not even provide the non-Communist nations of Indochina with the weapons to defend themselves from a Soviet-supported invasion.

The fracture of the post-war consensus has been along traditional isolationist-internationalist lines. But the pre-war roles have been reversed. Before Pearl Harbor and after Nagasaki, it was conservative Republicans who shared the Jeffersonian desire that there be "an ocean of fire between us and the old world." And it was the liberal Democrats who, like Daniel Webster a century before, deplored this parochial view, "The thunder, it may be said, rolls at a distance. The wide Atlantic is between us and danger: and however others may suffer *we* shall remain safe."[9]

Now, the torch has been passed. The conservatives of the Republican and Democratic Parties, and the anti-Communists of the AFL-CIO, stand in the foreign policy tradition of the post-war era. And it has been the liberal wing of the Democratic Party which has taken in, as an adopted son, the orphan of isolationism.

But something untraditional and new has been added. By the last days of American involvement in Vietnam, the Democratic left, and especially its allies among the men of words, had gone beyond jettisoning anti-Communism as a conviction, and containment as a policy. They had come to believe the United States had stumbled onto the wrong side of history, that America should break with the past and line herself up with the revolutionary tides rolling in from the left. No longer should the United States militarily oppose such revolutions. Rather, Washington should adopt a posture of indifference to Communist expansion, and of belligerence toward authoritarian regimes of the right, wherever they exist.

If one had to frame within a sentence what these Americans believe should be the objective of foreign policy it might run thus: The United States should concern itself less with resisting Communist-supported revolutions than with using its moral, diplomatic, economic and occasionally its military might to bring an end to racism, reaction and repression in those states with whom we have been too closely associated and too often allied.

They have indeed wandered out of history. By no stretch of the imagination is any rightist regime, from Brazil to Spain, from South Africa to South Korea, a threat to United States interests remotely approaching that reflected in the manifest purpose and military might of the U.S.S.R. To allow such a perception to shape policy is to allow ideology, not national interest, to dictate the course of the United States.

This body of intellectuals believes that—regardless of who is elected to office—its own perception of what is moral and immoral should prevail over any asserted pragmatic national interest of the United States. There is, quite simply, no realistic foreign policy the United States could pursue that would meet with their approval. That Dr. Kissinger was able, at times, to defang these critics is due to his brilliance and virtuosity, and not least to a unique capacity to sound like James Burnham in the Roosevelt Room and Joseph Kraft in Georgetown.

The *sécession des clercs* from the postwar consensus is not without great significance. For these intellectuals are too numerous, too vocal, too well placed to be ignored. Their rage, echoed in the press and politics, helped bring down Lyndon Johnson's government, and forced a reversal of war policy in the Far East. When the Nixon-Kissinger policies moved in their desired direction, i.e., the "Nixon Doctrine," the opening to China, detente with the Soviets—they were sullenly silent. When policy went the other way—as in Cambodia and Laos, and with the mining and bombing of the

North, they, their political associates and street auxiliaries could be relied upon to make of the White House a veritable hell for its occupants.

For the foreseeable future then the nation will be divided over foreign policy, and no matter the President—be he Ford, Rockefeller, Jackson, Muskie or Reagan—will have to anticipate their rancor and hostility. The future will be as Irving Kristol has predicted:

> . . . it is much to be doubted that the United States can continue to play an imperial role without the endorsement of its intellectual class. Or, to put it more precisely since there is no way the United States, as the world's mightiest power, can avoid such an imperial role, the opposition of its intellectuals means that this role will be played out in a domestic climate of ideological dissent that will enfeeble the resolution of our statesmen and diminish the credibility of their policies abroad.[10]

VI

In the final days of the nineteenth century, the Tsar of Russia, on learning that Austria was developing a new rapid firing cannon which the Romanovs lacked the technology and resources to match, called for an international peace conference to deal with a limitation of armaments. On hearing of this "lightning from the North," the British poet Rudyard Kipling sat down and penned "The Bear That Walks Like a Man." As recounted in Barbara Tuchman's classic, *The Proud Tower*, the poem "told a grim allegory of a man maimed and blinded when the bear he hunted stood up as if in supplication and the hunter 'touched with pity and wonder' witheld his fire only to have his face ripped away by the 'steel-shod paw.'"[11]

> When he stands up as pleading, in wavering, man-
> brute guise,

When he veils the hate and cunning of his little
   swinish eyes;
When he shows as seeking quarter, with paws like
   hands in prayer,
That is the time of peril—the time of the Truce
of the Bear! . . .

Kipling's doggerel is not without meaning for our own time.

Besides camaraderie and cordiality at the Summit, what has detente produced for the West? An arms agreement, muted Soviet response to the American mining of Haiphong and the December bombing of Hanoi, and the release of several tens of thousands of Soviet Jews to emigrate to Israel.

For the Soviets, detente has meant access to Western technology, investment and grain—while Soviet society remains quarantined from Western ideas. It has meant Western recognition of the changes made upon the map of Europe in 1945 by Stalin and the Red Army and recognition of the Soviet colony of East Germany, in exchange for guarantees not to interfere with Berlin. And it has meant a strategic arms agreemen under which the Soviet Union was left superior in missiles to the United States—and the Soviets allowed, without protest, to press to the limit every ambiguity in the text.

But there are other byproducts of detente. Under its warming breezes, Western states have shed their inhibitions about quarreling with one another and expressing publicly their distress with the arms burden. The Soviets have used the period to strengthen their legitimate claim to be the first military power on earth. Vis-à-vis the United States and the West, the Soviets are now in a more dominant position, militarily, than in 1968, and infinitely stronger than when Khrushchev approved the building of the Berlin Wall in 1961.

Nor has there been noticeable restraint in the adventurist and expansionist policies of Moscow. In 1968, along with their Warsaw Pact partners, the Soviets invaded Czechoslovakia, reestablished Communist orthodoxy, and asserted the unilateral right to intervene in any Socialist state where Communism was threatened. In 1969, if intelligence leaks had any validity, the Kremlin contemplated a preemptive strike against the embryonic nuclear installations of the PRC. In 1970, the Soviets fomented the Jordanian crisis. In 1972, Russian tanks and artillery fueled Hanoi's great spring offensive, when U.S. forces were at their most vulnerable—forcing the President to mine the harbors of the North—to prevent additional Russian arms from pouring in, weeks before the summit meeting in Moscow. In 1973, the Soviets were passive collaborators in the surprise attack on Israel. They rushed weapons and supplies to the war zone; they urged other Arab nations to join the fighting; they encouraged use of the oil weapon against the West; they threatened intervention with their own troops, when the tide shifted. In 1974, the only consistent thread in the changing Soviet policy regarding Cyprus was that it seemed designed to maximize hostility and conflict between those NATO allies. In 1975, it was Soviet equipment, poured into Haiphong in violation of the Paris Accords, which enabled Hanoi's armies to overrun the South, and inflict upon the United States its greatest foreign policy disaster since the fall of China in 1949. At the same time, Soviet diplomats were collaborating almost openly with Portuguese Communists and leftist military leaders, to split this NATO ally off from Europe and the West. The summit rhetoric, smiles and toasts aside, what is there in this pattern of behavior vastly different from Soviet conduct during the Cold War?

American officials, with heavy personal investments in detente, have been reluctant to condemn publicly these instances of Soviet belligerency and irresponsibility. Rather, as the alarmed protests pass through diplomatic channels, the appearances of understanding and cordiality are religiously maintained. In whose interest the continuing deceit?

Because of the overselling of detente, because the American people have been told endlessly that we are on the threshold of a "generation of peace," taxpayer willingness to pay for the arms which alone can guarantee peace and security evaporates.

So long as Mr. Khrushchev was banging his shoe and rattling his rockets, the West was united; and the Americans more than willing to make the sacrifices to keep at bay such an adversary. But now that Mr. Brezhnev speaks softly, even as he carries a bigger and bigger stick, that willingness disappears.

The "cold war rhetoric" may have been excessive. But assuredly, in assessing the character of our adversaries and the nature of the sacrifices we must make, it was a good deal more accurate and relevant than the toasts of detente. Indeed, if together with the Central Committee we are "building a structure of peace," and if alongside Mr. Mao and Mr. Chou we are taking a "long march" together, how does one then turn about and convince Americans of the need for warships, treaties and rockets to defend our Eastern hemisphere friends and allies against such as these?

VII

Here one touches upon an enduring dilemma of balance-of-power politics. While most Americans share John Quincy Adams' conviction that America does not go "abroad in search of monsters to destroy," they also believe with Adams that foreign policy must contain a moral content. The United States should side not only with nations with whom we share strategic interests but also with nations and peoples with whom we share common values, beliefs and institutions. Hence, Americans will more readily support the use of arms in causes portrayed as wars "to make the world safe for democracy," to "defend freedom," to defeat "Communist aggression." And they will not long countenance the spending of lives in a cause which appears without clear moral basis.

Louis XIV had stamped upon his cannon the inscription, *Ultima Ratio Regum*, the last argument of the king. Americans will approve of use of the last argument of the Republic, military force, to protect allies like Korea or Taiwan from invasion. They will not, however, to maintain a balance of power on the subcontinent, or to protect one set of Communists from overrunning another.

To the degree that U.S. policy statements downplay such values as freedom and liberty, and policy addresses are stripped of allusions to the evils and dangers of the Soviet and Chinese systems, and the irreconcilable differences between us, we undermine the arguments essential to convince Americans to make the sacrifices necessary to peace.

If Asian Communism is benign—the message that came off the Peking summit, uncontradicted by American foreign policy spokesmen—why *should* Americans risk war, and sacrifice billions of dollars and thousands of lives to prevent its absorption of Korea, Taiwan and Southeast Asia?

Balance-of-power politics can maintain the interest of intellectuals. It cannot inspire the sustained sacrifices of a democratic people. If Americans are not reminded that their far-flung armies and alliances are protecting what is right in this world, against the onslaught of what is malevolent, they will not long support a forward foreign policy, and the isolationism of the left will rapidly infect Middle America.

Through control of the press, the Communist system is able to insulate its subjects from the effects of endless utopian rhetoric about "peace, peace." Even as Soviet leaders hail detente in communications with the West, they preach vigilance and sacrifice to their own people.

"Peaceful co-existence does not mean the end of the struggle of the two world social systems," declared Pravda, August 22, 1973, in this era of detente. "The struggle between the proletariat and the bourgeoise, between world socialism and imperialism will be waged right up to the complete and final victory of Communism on a world scale."[12]

Western societies, however, are not so effectively quarantined from the diseases. Desirous as ever of an end to tension, anxiety and sacrifice, they tend to seize upon and take at face value the increasingly exaggerated claims of politicians and statesmen with a vested interest in detente.

But after all, what is detente, but "peaceful co-existence"

by another name, a period during which the ideological and political struggle proceeds apace, while a military truce is maintained, until the Communist world can emerge stronger than before. Like the Spirit of Geneva in 1955, the Spirit of Camp David in 1959, the Spirit of Moscow in 1963, and the Spirit of Holly Bush in 1967, detente is a passing, not a permanent, phase in East-West relations, from which the Soviets expect to emerge, first power upon earth.

VIII

What alternative has the right to the foreign policy of the present, the question is raised? A return to the public belligerence of the Cold War with the Soviets and Chinese?

The answer is no. The days when the threat of "rollback" and massive retaliation were credible have long since passed. The United States, no longer superior in arms, its freedom of action inhibited by Soviet power, has entered what author Richard Whalen has termed The Second Cold War. What the right has to offer America is essentially realism; it is the truth.

Several years ago, from within the Soviet Union, Aleksandr Solzhenitsyn wrote to the Nobel Prize Committee that:

. . . the spirit of Munich prevails in the twentieth century. The timid civilized world has found nothing with which to oppose the onslaught of a sudden revival of barefaced barbarity other than concessions and smiles.

The spirit of Munich is a sickness of the will of successful peoples. It is the daily condition of those who have given themselves up to the thirst after prosperity, at any price, to material well-being as the chief goal of earthly existence. Such people—and there are many in the world—elect passivity and retreat, just so as their accustomed life might drag on a bit longer, just so as not to step over the threshold of hardship today—and tomorrow, you'll see, it will be all right. (But it will never be all right! The price of cowardice will only be evil. We shall reap courage and victory only if we dare to make sacrifices.)[13]

What the West lacks so evidently and needs so desperately is the resolution, the will, the spirit of sacrifice in the defense of its civilization that the Israelis have shown in the defense of their homeland. The Communists are not invincible; they are not ten feet tall; their system is viewed with indifference or contempt by every people over whom it has seized power; their victory over the West is not inevitable, it is not written in stone.

What the West must overcome is its sense of defeatism, its sickness of the spirit. What it needs to recover is pride in its own civilization and achievements, and the self-confidence and missionary zeal that were hallmarks of the European and American peoples not too many decades ago. Finally, Westerners must cease this repeated and suicidal self-deception about the nature and purposes of their enemies, and regain the perspective to see the world as it is, not as we wish it to be.

If conservatives have a purpose it is to keep before the West the awareness that the days of sacrifice and hardship are not over, they have only just begun. It is in Roosevelt's phrase, "to speak the truth, the whole truth, frankly and boldly."

We have no evidence that the Soviets have abandoned the ideological or imperial objectives that informed the policies of Lenin, Stalin and Khrushchev. Soviet behavior from the Middle East to Southeast Asia, from the Kola Peninsula to Portugal to the Caribbean belies the contention that they share America's ambition of being a "partner in peace." The divisions and weakness of Western Europe and the oil of the Persian Gulf would be a temptation for any imperialist power, let alone one with the record of Soviet Russia.

The American people need to be made aware that the strategic superiority of the United States, and the traditional naval supremacy and freedom of action of the maritime nations of the West, belong to the past. America today is no less obligated, but less capable and willing than in 1960 to be, in John F. Kennedy's phrase, "watchmen on the walls of freedom."

And despite all the summit conferences and signed agreements, there remains the core of truth in what Karl Marx said a century ago, "There is only one way of dealing with a Power like Russia and this is the way of courage."

In the spring of 1975, Cambodia and South Vietnam, after having resisted longer and with higher casualties and as great a suffering as the American Confederacy, finally surrendered to Communist rule. They shared the fate visited in earlier decades upon Hungarians, Czechs and Poles, a fate that may one day soon come to Portuguese, Thais and the people of Berlin. Nearly a quarter century ago, Richard Weaver, the late conservative writer and philosopher of the South—the only region of America to know the immense tragedy of military defeat and occupation—foresaw that such a time of trouble might be coming, and he had some counsel for his countrymen:

> Belief in tragedy is essentially un-American; it is in fact one of the heresies against Americanism; but in the world as a whole this heresy is more widely received than the dogma and is more regularly taught by experience. Just as certainly as the United States grows older, it will have to find accommodation for this ineluctable notion; it is even now embarked upon policies with tremendous possibilities if not promises of tragedy. If we are in for a time of darkness and trouble, the Southern philosophy, because it is not based upon optimism, will have better power to console than the national dogmas.
>
> > It will do good to heart and head
> > when your soul is in my soul's stead.[14]

☆

Conservatism at the Crossroads

I

If conservatives would turn the nation around, they must set as their central political objective the capture of the Presidency.

Only the President has a podium of sufficient elevation, a microphone of adequate power, to rivet America's attention on issues the national press would otherwise ignore. Only the President can successfully block a Congress which has little control left of itself. Only the White House has the discipline and resources to conduct siege warfare against the bureaucracy. Only the President can transform the Supreme Court with Justices who will slam shut the book, belatedly, on this unfortunate era of government by decree.

And the Presidency remains the only repository of national authority and power remotely within reach of the right. For the present, Congress is a lost cause. As conservative thinker Jeffrey Hart has noted, an historic shift in perspectives has taken place. "If conservatives wish to get the 'executive branch' behind policies they deem desirable, they can do so only by supporting a powerful and activist Presidency."[1]

This potential menace to its political interests has not gone unnoticed on the left. Indeed, the intellectuals' assault on the "Imperial Presidency" has less to do with any principled aversion to concentrated power than to the sudden awakening that, with the nation moving rightward, the Presidency, that mighty instrument of government they helped forge, could be converted into a siege gun against the welfare state. Overnight, this realization transformed lifetime incense-burners like Arthur Schlesinger, Jr. into Cassandras warning of the Trojan Horse inside the Republic's walls.

The motives as well as the arguments of the academicians and essayists using Watergate to discredit the idea itself of a strong President and a powerful White House staff need to be inspected.

Watergate was not a failure of institutions; it was a crime of individuals. In yielding to media pressure, and down-grading his White House machinery, President Ford has ignored the principal instrument at his disposal to guarantee daily translation of his decisions into policy. What other instrument does the modern President have to monitor the bureaucracy, to impose constant discipline upon the agencies and departments of the sprawling federal government? Cabinet officers, no matter how loyal and reliable, are under constant pressures from special interests, the liberal press and the Congress. Even the most independent and able are partially beholden to a paper flow from civil servants, many of whom could not give a damn less what the voters of 49 states said in the last presidential election.

When President Ford declared, upon taking office, that decision-making authority was being restored to the Cabinet, when he voluntarily deeded his Domestic Council over to Nelson Rockefeller, there was general rejoicing in the capital. For the inmates would again be running the asylum; and the detested "Mandate of '72" would never be implemented.

Joseph Kraft's post-Christmas observation concerning the CIA has wide application: "There is no present threat to individual liberties from an all-powerful Executive. The reverse is true. The real danger is weakness at the center, bureaucrats playing to the press and the Congress, and demoralization all along the line."[2]

To effect a political counter-revolution in the capital—to which younger conservatives are committed—there is no substitute for a principled and dedicated Man of the Right in the Oval Office. Such a figure is the indispensable element of a conservative counter-reformation. Experience has shown a pragmatist cannot be counted upon to persevere in a goal in which he does not fully believe, in the face of the furious resistance that comes from the vested interests in Congress, the bureaucracy, the media and the courts.

Unquestionably, a working majority on the Hill would make the task easier. But without that man in the Oval Office, the thousands of sweetheart contracts between the federal government and the new "poverty-education industrial complex" will never be scrapped. The new priorities—shifting wealth away from the consuming sector of society back to the producers—will never be imposed upon the revenue code. And the long overdue confrontation between an elected government, and an appointive federal judiciary, hell-bent on remaking society through court decree, will never occur.

To look to the present, or any conceivable Congress in the immediate future, for such leadership is to look in vain.

The Congress of the United States, the home of Webster, Calhoun and Clay is, as Joseph Alsop commented at retirement, hip-deep in pygmies. No one in Washington expects other than that, faced with the choice between what is popular and what is painful and necessary, Congress will agree enthusiastically on the former. There will be no cuts in social spending, despite a budget running *a billion and a half dollars a week* into debt. There will be no 5-percent ceiling on new federal pay raises, or social security benefits. The Congress has not only lost control of the budget; it has lost control of itself. We have moved out of the era when Capitol Hill could be counted upon to check the excesses of an ambitious President into an era when Congress must constantly be watched like some delinquent child, lest it vote another slice of the nation's wealth, to purchase itself yet another voting bloc for the next election.

After observing the Ninety-fourth Congress in operation a single month, *National Review* raised a question, which has not yet satisfactorily been answered:

> Not all Congressmen react this way . . . But enough of them in this new and more urbane but essentially Mc-Governite Congress have so reacted to the President's call for remedial action as to raise the question: has it become impossible, in the United States, for democratically elected legislators to take the harsh measures needed for survival? Are their terms of office so short, have modern communications made them so vulnerable to retaliation from their constituents, the media, and the special interest lobbies, that they have—or they feel they have—little choice but to choose the instant nostrum rather than the hard and sustained regime that a profligate nation must undergo before it can be restored to economic health?[3]

Once raised, the question pointed the editor toward a conclusion others are reaching:

"As we look across the Atlantic to Europe . . . and see nation after nation there ruled by paper-thin majorities or unstable, awkward coalitions, one wonders whether democracy as it has developed in the third quarter of the twentieth century can long survive."

II

A powerful undertow of constituent and media pressure is carrying Congress out to sea. Only the President can stand against it. Is Gerald R. Ford the man?

Certainly, his performance in office has shown him not without courage.

But of him, and his Michigan and Hill cohorts, it may

fairly be said: they never fought for the Presidency; they never forged a national victory; they feel no obligation to the mandate President Nixon's men believed they had won. Indeed, few of them dreamed they would ever be where they are today. "I never in a million years thought I'd end up here," the President unabashedly told the *Washington Post*. Like some brash Fortinbras with his retinue arriving in the final scene of *Hamlet,* to take charge of the disposition of affairs, the President and his Hill and Michigan counselors appear at times not even to understand what the bloodshed and carnage were about.

The age of Eisenhower and Kennedy is over, finished, gone. The postwar consensus on American foreign policy shattered irreparably on Vietnam. It cannot be restored. Political divisions over economic and social policy are as broad and deep as in the thirties. In 1975, there can be no successful politics of "communication, conciliation, compromise and co-operation." How does one split-the-difference between those delighted the United States washed it hands of Indochina and those who believed that both the national interest and a moral obligation dictated that we help our allies in their death agony?

In its convention of 1972 and the Congress of 1975, the Democratic Party has chosen its course. It has opted for equality before freedom, for socialism over capitalism, for neo-isolationism, and the steady withdrawal of American participation in the anti-Communist alliances of the fifties.

The national Republicans, however, have not yet decided irrevocably where they stand on the issues of the new era. The party wishes to be thought of as both "principled" and "progressive." It prefers the more comfortable, less bitter conflicts of an earlier age. Its leader is not a politician of the seventies, but a product of the fifties; he belongs to the age of Eisenhower and Kennedy, when there was national unity over American foreign policy, bipartisan cooperation between liberals and conservatives, once we reached the water's edge.

The longer Mr. Ford attempts to cast himself as leader of all the people, the longer he delays in placing himself at the head of the anti-McGovern coalition in American politics, the greater the likelihood that other men and other institutions will emerge.

Mr. Nixon's landslide was a vote of protest as well as affirmation, a vote against everything George McGovern represented to the working and middle class—higher taxes for social spending, expanded welfare, reductions in defense, reverse discrimination favoring the fashionable minorities, bussing to integrate the schools, permissiveness on social issues and appeasement in Asia. The nation did not vote to go halfway with Mr. McGovern. It voted to reject him in the greatest landslide won by a genuine Republican in history.

If Mr. Ford's reluctant warriors determine that their guiding principle should be to take those actions least displeasing to the greatest number, if their objective is to enjoy as long as possible the unanticipated gift of the gods, then their claim upon the conservatives is nonexistent. The right needs to be dealt a hand in the politics of 1976; if the President is unwilling to play that hand, someone else should be seated at the table.

III

In the summer of 1975, with only the President a certain candidate in the Republican primaries, it is still too early, by seasons, for conservatives to chart any final course for the summer and fall of 1976. But clearly, as the situation is new, so it is time to think and act anew.

The possibility exists, as Mr. Nixon would have put it, that the "Republican Party has broken its pick." In 1972, the Republicans went before the nation as the party of "peace with honor," and the spokesman of Middle America against the liberal elite; it swept forty-nine states. In 1974, the Republicans went to the country with an appeal, as one wag put it, "half-Hoover and half-Harding." The grotesque Ninety-fourth Congress is a consequence.

Millions of Democrats who voted Republican in 1972 were

hit by Watergate in 1973, double-digit inflation in 1974, and a near depression in 1975. One will not make many converts if, after the first instructions, the postulant is beaten and robbed as he leaves the rectory. Many Democrats are ashamed of the vote they cast in 1972; they will not easily be convinced to vote Republican again.

Nationally, Republican identification is beginning to disappear. According to Gallup, Democratic identification is at 44 percent, Independents at 33 percent and Republicans at 23 percent. Other polls show the party down to 18 percent. Among the young, the figures are worse still. As more and more Americans identify themselves as "conservatives," fewer and fewer associate themselves with the Republican Party. The hour may be approaching for conservatives to dissolve a popular front with the Republican Party that no longer seems to serve their political interests.

But if the political battalions and generals of '76 remain unknown, the issues do not. Come 1976, this nation may be facing a grave economic situation. If so, it will be the result not of conservative policies, but of liberal policies. And the right should make clear to the country, in 1975, that the fiscal policy being pursued in Washington by the Administration and the Congress, is done against the protest of the right. Conservatives should behave politically as what they are— strangers to the corridors of power, dissenters outside the councils of government, men without power and without responsibility for what is happening in this capital.

While the economic issue remains paramount, the other issues of '72 remain extant and exploitable.

On these issues, the right should make sharp, clear and public its deep and fundamental disagreements with both the Democratic Congress and the Republican Administration. The Holt Amendment, which, at a stroke, might have stripped HEW of the capacity to impose racial balance on the public schools, failed only because the White House conspired in its defeat.

Conservatives should begin to view themselves as temporary allies of the GOP, not foot soldiers in the ranks. If there was a failure of conservatives in the Nixon years, it was not that they were too independent, but that they were too loyal.

IV

Looking toward 1976, and beyond, the right should reexplore the battlefields of 1972. In the "new majority" mustered together by President Nixon remains the constituent elements of conservative victory.

Holding his Republican base secure, the President registered his gains among Democrats and Independents with the three-to-one majorities amassed in the Old Confederacy, and with over half of the enormous Catholic and ethnic vote of the big cities. It was an alliance of the Republican base from 1968, a modest contingent of Humphrey bread-and-butter Democrats, and an army of Wallace people.

Yet, the party that made these historic inroads in 1972, among Northern Irish and Italians and Southern Protestants, was by 1974 busy fashioning a "positive action" program to guarantee proportional representation at future conventions for blacks, Chicanos, Indians and feminists. It would be difficult to imagine four voting blocs less receptive to the Republican Party philosophy. For the GOP to be toying with such alien concepts, which led to the Democratic debacle at Miami Beach, is but one symptom that the party really has lost its bearings. There are others.

Last fall, one Republican Governor of a major state pronounced himself publicly dismayed with the "immorality" of a "Southern Strategy" which swept Dixie, lock, stock and barrel, into the Republican column in 1972. All this suggests something sadder than simply Republicans parroting the editorials of the Eastern press. It suggests that, in their hearts, many Republicans truly believe that quotas, and "affirmative action" schemes, compulsory integration and the Dixie-baiting of the national Democrats are the proper political course, for moral reasons.

The sentiment is Gadarene in destination. There is no conceivable way the Republican Party can remain true to its principles and compete effectively with the Democratic Party for the votes of blacks or other minorities who look for advancement to federal authority, federal programs and federal power.

Every armchair strategist knows that to win, Republicans —with their numerical inferiority—must go poaching on the Democratic preserve. But, as Senator Goldwater said, you go hunting where the ducks are. For Republicans, the Democratic ducks are in South Boston, and they are roosting all over Dixie. There are next to none in Manhattan and Harlem, but hundreds of thousands in Queens and the North Bronx.

Not only are the Catholic Democrats of Queens more numerous than the black Democrats of Harlem, they are more disillusioned with their party, and receptive to a political appeal that does not violate Republican principles. If to be fashionable we must devise affirmative action programs, then let us discriminate in favor of the Democratic minorities we can win—conservative Jews and Catholics in the Northeast, and working-class and rural Protestants from the border states and Deep South.

As Senators Goldwater and McGovern both demonstrated, there is, in a two-way national race, a floor under the national vote of the Republican and Democratic candidate, near 40 percent.

That leaves the decision, every four years, in the hands of twenty percent of the electorate. This "swing vote"—the Republican National Committee should keep in mind—is not a black vote; it is not a Chicano vote; it is not an Indian vote; it is not a vote which can be delivered by Betty Friedan. It was, by and large in 1968 and 1972, a Wallace vote—an angry, alienated, turned-off, working- and middle-class vote which, like Tex Ritter's "boll weevil," is "lookin' for a home, jes' lookin' for a home." One alienates, not attracts, this vote, by prefabricating the kind of multi-lingual polyglot convention that will pass muster with the League of Women Voters and Common Cause.

That the conservative "majority" gathered in 1972 is "out

there" seems certain. That the Republican Party can again bring it together is doubtful. The historic opportunity, first presented to the Republicans in 1968, to become the party of the emerging majority in American politics—seemingly realized in 1972—may finally have passed away. The issues endure. Yet, how does the Republican Party after eight years in office, exploit them?

After two Republican Presidents have shoved the nation $180 billion deeper in debt, how does one make the case for fiscal prudence? After all our anti-bussing rhetoric, where were we when the crunch came in Denver and South Boston? How does the Party of Watergate make the law-and-order appeal? What do we say about a crime rate that has risen as rapidly in the Republican years as in the sixties? How does the party of limited government explain funding the Great Society?

One recalls all those press clippings of '69 about our having caught the liberals swimming, and stolen off with their clothes. Well how do they fit now—going into 1976?

On countless issues the conservative side remains the convincing case. People yet want a military defense second to none, a reduced tax burden, a halt to the deficits that produce inflation, and ultimately, recession. They want an end to government favoritism toward the welfare class. They want religion and discipline restored to their public schools and value-free sex education and Eldridge Cleaver thrown out. They are rightly bitter about government-imposed racial quotas and reverse discrimination. They are visceral about bureaucrats and judges using their children to meet an arbitrary racial balance in a school halfway across a dangerous city. They want the more effective measures they never seem to get against pornography, crime and drugs. They have only contempt for those permissive judges who live in the distant and secure suburbs and lecture the community on the long-range benefits of court leniency. They are contemptuous, too, of the environmental extremists more alarmed over Atlantic fish and Alaskan caribou than the jobs of auto workers or the economic independence of the United States. And they have had a bellyful of militants of all shades and stripes who dominate the airwaves with their endless belly-aching about how badly they are mistreated and what a rotten country this is. There is a constituency, "out there," responsive to a conservative appeal. The question is whether it will ever again listen to the Republican Party.

V

What strategy does the right pursue?

The first of the available options, the most likely in the late spring of 1975, is for the former Governor of California, Ronald Reagan, to make the conservative demonstration against the President in the Republican primaries in the spring of 1976. That course carries with it a significant opportunity for success at the Republican convention—but only a slim chance of victory in the fall.

Whatever criticisms may be made of Gerald Ford's economic and social policies ("I try to be conservative whenever I can"), his Republican passport is stamped and in good order. He deserves well of the party to which he has paid his dues for twenty-six years. A primary challenge against him can have but two outcomes. It can fail, forcing Republican conservatives to back a weakened moderate Republican in the fall. Or it can succeed in denying the President of the United States the nomination of his own party.

But how would repudiation by Republicans of their own President, at his own national convention, sit with those party and precinct workers who like and respect Gerald R. Ford? How would rejection of their Administration affect the attitudes, in the election, of the President and Vice President of the United States? How does one run at the top of the Republican ticket, and make an effective case against policies which Republican administrations have themselves pursued for eight years? Gained at such a price, what would the GOP nomination be worth?

The answer is next to nothing—especially if George Wallace has decided to make a third party challenge from the right.

Ergo, the decision to challenge Gerald Ford in the primaries must carry with it another commitment—to make common cause with the Wallace wing of the Democratic Party, should the nomination be won.

Despite its sudden enthusiasm for loyalty oaths, the liberal wing of the Republican Party, and a significant segment of its moderate wing, would walk out of a national convention which dumped the President for a candidate like Ronald Reagan. Unless the right wing of the GOP then sought out a coalition with the right wing of the Democratic Party, the result in 1976 would be a replay of 1964.

There is a second possibility which cannot be dismissed. It is that President Ford, for reasons personal or political, will step down in 1976. Like Lyndon Johnson, he will decline to run. In such an event, conservatives, the traditional grass roots power of the GOP, would be favored to capture the nomination and write the platform.

But again, the questions arise: Of what value a Republican nomination in 1976, if a sitting President is unwilling to fight for it? And though the GOP nomination can customarily guarantee a candidate 40 percent of the national vote in a two-way race, will the social conservatives who voted for George Wallace in the spring of 1972 and Nixon-Agnew in the fall again pull the lever for the party that brought them Watergate and hard times.

And, again, a conservative sweep of the Republican primaries of 1976 carries with it the genuine possibility of a liberal walkout in the fall.

What both "scenarios" point to then is this: If the conservatives go the road of the Republican primaries, they must anticipate a party split at the convention; and they must seek out a political alliance with the Wallace Democrats, for the fall, or they will go down to the worst conservative defeat since November of 1964. The Wallace supporters are the indispensable element of any conservative-Republican strategy in 1976. Without them, the Republican right does not stand a

chance. With them, political realignment becomes a proba-
bility and recapture of the White House a possibility in 1975.

There is a third possibility. It is that, come the late fall of
1975, the President will realize that not only his political
future, but the national interest, dictates that he declare war
on the Congress, on behalf of conservative principles and
policies. By the fall of 1975, Gerald Ford may be waging
political war against the Ninety-fourth Congress in the relentless style of FDR and Harry Truman. Should that come
to pass, should the President by the fall be making the conservative demonstration on issues, foreign and domestic, conservatives may well conclude they have no other reasonable
alternative than to support him—and redirect their attention
to the party platform, the Vice-Presidency and 1980. If Gerald Ford is not Edmund Burke, he is not Edmund Muskie
either. And if the choice is reduced to the President or any
candidate the modern Democratic Party would nominate,
there is no choice.

The final course to consider is the "third party option,"
the independent conservative ticket for President, running
free of and against the slates of both national parties.

The objective would not only be the capture of the Presidency, but the realignment of the nation's political parties,
the forging of a new unity between the economic conservatives of the Republican party and the social conservatives of
the Democratic Party. It would be to erect a new political
tent to contain both William F. Buckley, Jr., listening to the
C-Sharp Minor of Rachmaninoff, and George Corley Wallace's people, listening to Hank Williams.

There are deterrents, however, and dangers in such a step.
First, for the Republican right to abandon the GOP in 1976
is to abandon it forever. Never strike a king unless you kill
him, Mr. Nixon used to say. If conservatives pursue a course
in 1976 designed to defeat the Republican President for election in his own right, they should not expect to be welcomed
home to their father's house in January of 1977. The lot of
the defector in American politics is not an attractive one. And
before conservatives write off as useless the party they cap-

tured in 1964 and have controlled since, they ought to inspect more closely the asset they seem so willing to throw away.

Secondly, if there is to be a merger between the conservative wings of both parties in 1976, it is a certitude, almost, that the senior partner in the new firm will be George Wallace the Democrat, not Ronald Reagan, nor any other Republican. The American party which controls the ballot position in many states looks to George Wallace and no one else as its natural leader in the fall of 1976.

Next, conservatives should be aware that the most likely outcome of a strong "third party" challenge is the defeat of the second and third parties—and the election of a liberal Democrat as President of the United States. With Nelson Rockefeller or Elliott Richardson or Charles Percy the Republican nominee, a third-party enterprise might be viable. But with President Ford at the top of the ticket, the conservatives in 1976 would likely be divided and defeated.

Finally, the heart has reasons that the mind knows not. For conservatives who have long been loyal to the GOP, who believe deeply in the continuity of institutions, it would be a wrenching experience to abandon and attack the party of their youth, their hopes, their dreams.

Perhaps, when the crunch comes in the summer of 1976, there may be no other choice, consistent with conservative convictions. But if so, the step should not be taken until a more conclusive prognosis has been made that the Republican Party is indeed sick unto death, no longer a seaworthy vessel of the new conservatism.

Yet, such a step cannot be ruled out. For neither party today voices the concerns or defends the interests of the hardest working and most productive of citizens. Both parties are up to their elbows in this sordid business of bidding for votes with the tax dollars of the American people. And things need saying that are not being said.

Notes

Introduction

1. Senator Barry Goldwater, *The Conscience of a Conservative* (Shepherdsville, Kentucky: Victor Publishing Company, Inc., 1960) p. 28.
2. Bertrand de Jouvenel, "The Treatment of Capitalism by Continental Intellectuals," *Capitalism and the Historians,* edited by F. A. Hayek (Chicago: University of Chicago Press, 1954) p. 103.
3. Norman Mailer, *Miami and the Siege of Chicago* (New York: The New American Library, 1968) p. 51.

Why Liberalism Prevails

1. In *Nixon on the Issues*, published by the Nixon-Agnew Campaign Committee, October 17, 1968.
2. Justice William O. Douglas, *Points of Rebellion*. In Ben Wattenberg, *The Real America* (Garden City, New York: Doubleday, 1974) p. 28.
3. George F. Will, "Life in 'Conspicuous Washington'," *The Washington Post*, December 31, 1974.

4. Jeffrey Hart, "Reagan-Wallace: Middle Class Populism," *The Manchester Union-Leader*, November 21, 1974, p. 43.

5. Jeffrey Hart, "The Presidency: Shifting Conservative Perspectives," *The National Review*, November 22, 1974, p. 1355.

6. Irving Kristol, "What Comes Next After Watergate," *The Wall Street Journal*, June 14, 1973.

Capitalism and the Intellectuals

1. Lewis F. Powell, Jr., "Confidential Memorandum, Attack on American Free Enterprise," to Mr. Edwin B. Sydnor, Jr., Chairman, Education Committee, U.S. Chamber of Commerce, August 23, 1971 (Provided by U.S. Chamber of Commerce, Washington, D.C.).

2. Edmund Burke, *Reflections on the Revolution in France*. Introduction by Russell Kirk (New Rochelle: Arlington House) p. 124.

3. Two above paragraphs drawn considerably, especially quotations, from Will Durant's, *The Story of Philosophy* (New York: Washington Square Press, 1952) pp. 218, 231.

4. Irving Kristol, "American Intellectuals and Foreign Policy," *On the Democratic Idea in America* (New York: Harper & Row, 1972) p. 69.

5. Bertrand de Jouvenel, "The Treatment of Capitalism by Continental Intellectuals," *Capitalism and the Historians*, edited by F. A. Hayek (Chicago: Chicago University Press, 1954) pp. 120, 121.

6. Eric Hoffer, *The Ordeal of Change* (New York: Harper & Row, 1964) pp. 50, 51.

7. Irving Kristol, *Commentary*, November, 1972. In *The Wall Street Journal* editorial, "The 'New Class'," December 21, 1972.

8. Dr. Benjamin A. Rogge, "Will Capitalism Survive?" *Imprimis* (Hillsdale, Michigan: Hillsdale College, 1974). *Note:* For this discussion of Schumpeter's ideas, considerable debt is owed to the May, 1974 presentation by Dr. Rogge at Hillsdale. His exegesis is worth reading in its entirety.

9. Kevin Phillips, "The Populist Alliance," December 16, 1974. Column syndicated by King Features, New York, N.Y.

10. William Raspberry, "What's Ahead for the Poor." *The Washington Post,* November 29, 1974.
11. Lewis F. Powell, Jr., *op. cit.* (see Note 1, this Chapter).
12. Herman Kahn, "Kahnversation: An Interview with Jonathan Ward," *Intellectual Digest,* September, 1972.
13. Edith Efron, "The Free Mind and the Free Market," delivered at Pepperdine University's Business-Education-Media Seminar, Malibu, California, May 9, 1974. *Vital Speeches,* July 15, 1974, p. 523.

On Integration and Education

1. *Twenty Years After Brown: Equality of Educational Opportunity,* A report of the U.S. Commission on Civil Rights, March, 1975 (Second in a Series) p. 46.
2. James J. Kilpatrick, "Turning the Constitution on Its Head," November 15–16, 1969. Column syndicated by *Washington Star Syndicate, Inc.* New York, N.Y.
3. *The Washington Star,* editorial, May 27, 1968.
4. Alexander M. Bickel, "Where Do We Go from Here," *The New Republic,* February 7, 1970, p. 18.
5. David Gumbert, "Unwelcome Recess: Boston Busing Dispute Disrupts the Education and Lives of Students," *The Wall Street Journal,* April 7, 1975, p. 1.
6. Jenkin Lloyd Jones, "The Academic Carrot and Stick," *The Detroit News,* October 18, 1974. (Column distributed by the *Los Angeles Times Syndicate.*)
7. Juan Cameron, "Chaos and Decay," *The Washington Star,* March 30, 1975 (reprinted from March 1975 issue of *Fortune*).
8. Walter Mossberg, "Mr. Chips at the Polling Booth," *The Wall Street Journal,* October 21, 1974, p. 12.
9. *Note:* For this Part VI discussion of the Forest Hills project, considerable debt is owed to the *Village Voice,* January 6, 1972, and the excellent piece entitled "The Torah and the Torch," by Clark Whelton.
10. *The Autobiography of Malcolm X* (New York: Grove Press, 1966) p. 344. In Edward Banfield's *The Unheavenly City, The Nature and Future of Our Urban Crisis* (Boston: Little, Brown) p. 67.

11. Alexander M. Bickel, *The Supreme Court and the Idea of Progress* (New York: Harper & Row, 1970) p. 17.

Can Democracy Survive the New Journalism?

1. Theodore H. White, *The Making of the President 1972* (New York: Atheneum, 1973) p. 245.
2. Douglass Cater, *The Fourth Branch of Government* (Boston: Houghton Mifflin, 1959).
3. Dr. Ernest K. Lefever, *TV and National Defense, An Analysis of CBS News, 1972–1973* (Boston, Virginia: Institute for American Strategy Press, 1974) pp. 26–31, 36, 41–42, 53, 103, 127.
4. Walter Cronkite, an interview carried by *Gannett News Service*, published in the Utica (N.Y.) Press, reported in the January 1975 issue of *Centernews*, a publication of Institute for American Strategy, Boston, Virginia.
5. The Holy Bible, The Acts of the Apostles, 17:21.
6. William Safire, *Before the Fall* (Garden City, N.Y.: Doubleday, 1975) p. 173.
7. Thomas Jefferson, "Letter to Horatio G. Spafford, March 17, 1814." In *Bartlett's Familiar Quotations*, Thirteenth and Centennial Edition (Boston: Little, Brown, 1955) p. 375.

The Distribution of Wealth

1. John Kenneth Galbraith, in Ben J. Wattenberg, *The Real America* (Garden City, N.Y.: Doubleday, 1974) p. 33.
2. Robert M. Bleiberg, "Editorial Commentary," *Barron's*, August 19, 1974, p. 7.
3. "The Transfer Payment Explosion," *The Wall Street Journal*, January 24, 1975, p. 10.
4. John F. Kennedy, the *Boston Post*, April 23, 1950. In Dr. Roger A. Freeman, *The Growth of American Government: A Morphology of the Welfare State* (Stanford: Hoover Institution Press, 1975) p. 158.

5. Richard Weaver, *The Southern Tradition at Bay, A History of Postbellum Thought*. Forward by Donald Davidson (New Rochelle, N.Y.: Arlington House, 1968) p. 18.
6. Leo Barnes, "One Way to End the Bear Market," *The Wall Street Journal*, October 9, 1974.
7. Albert Shanker, quoted by David Halberstam, "The Very Expensive Education of McGeorge Bundy," *Harper's Magazine*, July, 1969, p. 40.
8. McGeorge Bundy, in "Why Big Foundations are Hurting for Cash," *U.S. News & World Report*, November 18, 1974, p. 56.

Economic and Social Policy

1. Otto Eckstein, *The New York Times*, December 29, 1974. In Nicholas Von Hoffman column, *The Washington Post*, January 13, 1975.
2. "The Debt Economy," In Special Issue of *Business Week*, October 12, 1974, p. 45.
3. Franklin D. Roosevelt, Message to Congress, January 4, 1935: *Public Papers*, IV, 19 (Source: *Treasury of Presidential Quotations*, Harsberger, p. 270).
4. Roger A. Freeman, "The Wayward Welfare State." An Address to the 56th Annual Conference, Governmental Research Association, September 1, 1970, Chicago. (Dr. Freeman is Senior Fellow at the Hoover Institution on War, Revolution and Peace at Stanford University.)
5. Jeffrey Hart, "Hunger in America—And Politics," *Indianapolis Star*, February 17, 1971.
6. *Note:* Quotations from John Gardner, Senator Muskie, Senator Mondale and Gary Hart were taken from Ben Wattenberg's *The Real America*, op. cit., pp. 28, 31, 32.
7. *Note:* Most of the statistics herein were taken either from *Social Indicators*, 1973, a publication of the Office of Management and Budget, or from Mr. Wattenberg's previously cited work, *The Real America*. Both are invaluable sources of data on the material advances made by the vast majority of Americans over the past third of a century.

Beyond Detente

1. "What Happens Next in the Mideast," *The Washington Post*, page A-30, November 21, 1974.
2. C. L. Sulzberger, "Signposts to Disaster," *The New York Times*, October 30, 1974.
3. Andrew J. Pierre, "America Down, Russia Up: The Changing Political Role of Military Power," *Foreign Policy*, Fall, 1971, p. 182.
4. Richard J. Whalen, *Taking Sides: A Personal View of America from Kennedy to Nixon to Kennedy* (Boston: Houghton Mifflin, 1974) p. 288.
5. C. L. Sulzberger, "Decolonialism Amok?," *The New York Times*, January 22, 1975.
6. V. I. Lenin, Speech to Commissars of Education, Moscow, 1923.
7. John Dornberg, "Soviet Union: A Melting Pot That Simmers" (written from Munich), *The Washington Star*, January 8, 1975.
8. Walter Lippmann, *U.S. Foreign Policy: Shield of the Republic* (Boston: Little, Brown, 1943) p. 3.
9. Both the Jefferson and Webster quotations are taken from Foster Rhea Dulles, *America's Rise to World Power 1898–1954* (New York: Harper & Row, 1954) pp. 7, 10.
10. Irving Kristol, *On the Democratic Idea in America* (New York: Harper & Row, 1972) p. 83. (From "American Intellectuals and Foreign Policy" which originally appeared in *Foreign Affairs*, July 1967.)
11. Barbara W. Tuchman, *The Proud Tower* (New York: Macmillan, 1966) p. 230.
12. *Pravda*, August 22, 1973. (From Leon Gouré, Foy D. Kohler, Mose L. Harvey, *The Role of Nuclear Forces in Current Soviet Strategy* (Center for Advanced International Studies, University of Miami, 1974) p. xxii.
13. Aleksandr I. Solzhenitsyn, on Receiving the 1970 Nobel Prize for Literature, *The New York Times*, August 25, 1972.
14. Richard M. Weaver, *The Southern Tradition at Bay*, op. cit. p. 14 (See Chapter V, No. 5.)

Conservatism at the Crossroads

1. Jeffrey Hart, "The Presidency: Shifting Conservative Perspectives," *The National Review*, November 22, 1974, p. 1353.
2. Joseph Kraft, "The Colby Case," *The Washington Post*, December 26, 1974.
3. *National Review Bulletin*, February 7, 1975, p. B13.